Collins

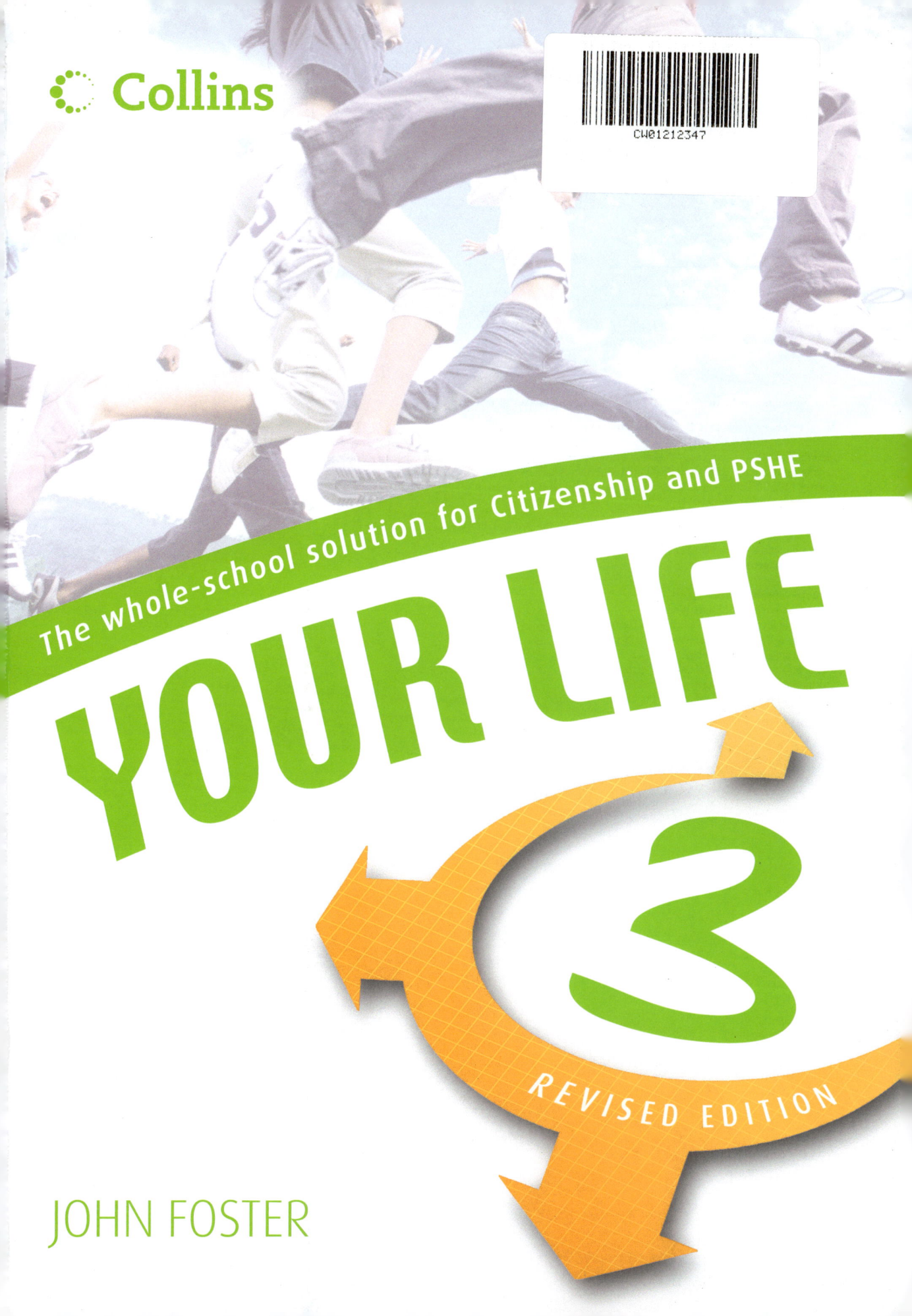

The whole-school solution for Citizenship and PSHE

YOUR LIFE 3

REVISED EDITION

JOHN FOSTER

William Collins' dream of knowledge for all began with the publication of his first book in 1819. A self-educated mill worker, he not only enriched millions of lives, but also founded a flourishing publishing house. Today, staying true to his spirit, Collins books are packed with inspiration, innovation and practical expertise. They place you at the centre of a world of possibility and give you exactly what you need to explore it.

Collins. Do more.

Published by Collins
An imprint of HarperCollinsPublishers
77–85 Fulham Palace Road
Hammersmith
London
W6 8JB

Browse the complete Collins catalogue at
www.collinseducation.com

© HarperCollinsPublishers Limited 2005

10 9 8 7 6 5 4 3 2 1

ISBN 0 00 719852 3

John Foster asserts his moral right to be identified as the author of this work.

All rights reserved. No part of this publication may be reproduced, stored in a retrieval system, or transmitted in any form or by any means, electronic, mechanical, photocopying, recording or otherwise, without the prior written permission of the Publisher or a licence permitting restricted copying in the United Kingdom issued by the Copyright Licensing Agency Ltd., 90 Tottenham Court Road, London W1T 4LP.

British Library Catalogue in Publication Data
A catalogue record for this publication is available from the British Library.

Commissioned by Thomas Allain-Chapman
Project management by Gaynor Spry
Edited by Kim Richardson
Editorial assistant: Charlie Evans
Picture research by Suzanne Williams
Design and layout by Ken Vail Graphic Design, Cambridge
Illustrations by Bethan Matthews (p43), David Mitchell (p54)
Cover design by bluepigdesign
Cover photographs: Pixland/Bruno Coste
Production by Katie Butler
Printed and bound by Printing Express Ltd, Hong Kong

Contents

Introducing *Your Life*   4

1. **You and your body** – adolescence   6
2. **You and your responsibilities** – racism, prejudice and discrimination   10
3. **You and your decisions** – how to make decisions   16
4. **You and your family** – becoming an adult   20
5. **You and your values** – human rights issues   24
6. **You and your feelings** – dealing with loss   30
7. **You and your body** – drugs and drugtaking   34
8. **You and the law** – crimes and punishments   38
9. **You and other people** – being assertive   44
10. **You and the media** – the power of the press   48
11. **You and your money** – banking and ways of saving   52
12. **You and your body** – eating disorders   56
13. **You and the community** – local government and local organisations   60
14. **You and your opinions** – which political party do you support?   64
15. **You and your body** – safer sex, STIs and AIDS   68
16. **You as a citizen** – of the world   72
17. **You and the community** – pressure groups and campaigning   78
18. **You and other people** – people with mental illnesses   82
19. **You and global issues** – poverty   88
20. **You and your achievements** – reviewing your progress   94

Index   96

Introducing *Your Life*

Your Life 3 is the third of three books which together form a comprehensive course in Personal, Social and Health Education, and Citizenship at Key Stage 3. This table shows how the twelve PSHE units and eight Citizenship units cover the requirements of the National Framework for PSHE and the National Curriculum Programme of Study for Citizenship.

Personal, Social and Health Education

	Understanding Yourself	**Keeping Healthy**	**Developing Relationships**
	These units concentrate on developing your self-knowledge and your ability to manage your emotions, to make decisions and to manage your money.	These units are designed to complement the work on health education that you are doing elsewhere in the curriculum.	These units aim to develop your ability to handle close relationships in your dealings with other people in the community.
Your Life 1	• You and your feelings – anxieties and worries • You and your time – managing your time • You and your money – pocket money, budgeting and saving • You and your achievements – reviewing your progress	• You and your body – growing and changing • You and your body – smoking • You and your body – eating and exercise • You and your body – drugs and drugtaking	• You and your family – getting on with others • You and other people – bullying • You and your responsibilities – beliefs, customs and festivals • You and other people – people with disabilities
Your Life 2	• You and your feelings – self-esteem • You and your time – making the most of your leisure • You and your money – gambling • You and your achievements – reviewing your progress	• You and your body – drinking and alcohol • You and your body – contraception and sex • You and your safety – at home and in the street • You and your body – drugs and drugtaking	• You and your family – divided families • You and other people – friends and friendships • You and your responsibilities – other cultures and lifestyles • You and other people – older people
Your Life 3	• You and your feelings – dealing with loss (PSHE 1d, 3c, 3e) • You and your decisions – how to make decisions (PSHE 1a, 3i, 3j) • You and your money – banking and ways of saving (PSHE 1g/Citizenship 2c) • You and your achievements – reviewing your progress (PSHE 1a/Citizenship 3c)	• You and your body – adolescence (PSHE 1a, 1c, 1d, 2a, 2c, 3e) • You and your body – safer sex and STDs/AIDS (PSHE 2e) • You and your body – eating disorders (PSHE 2b, 2f) • You and your body – drugs and drugtaking (PSHE 2d, 2h)	• You and your family – becoming an adult (PSHE 3e, 3g, 3h, 3i, 3k) • You and other people – being assertive (PSHE 1b, 1c, 3a, 3i, 3k) • You and your responsibilities – tolerance, prejudice and discrimination (Citizenship 1b, 2a, 3a/ PSHE 3a, 3b, 3j, 3k) • You and other people – people with mental illnesses (PSHE 2c)

The various activities within each unit provide opportunities for you to learn how to grow as individuals, for example, by developing self-awareness and taking responsibility for managing your time. The group discussion activities involve you in learning how to co-operate and negotiate. You are presented with situations in which you have to work with others, to analyse information, to consider moral and social dilemmas and to make choices and decisions.

Citizenship

Developing as a citizen

These units aim to develop your knowledge and understanding of the world around you, and to develop the skills that you will require as active citizens.

Your Life 1
- You and the law – children's rights
- You and the community – being a good neighbour
- You as a citizen – Britain's government
- You and the media – the power of television
- You and your opinions – how to express your ideas
- You and your values – right and wrong
- You and global issues – resources, waste and recycling
- You and the community – taking action: raising money for a charity

Your Life 2
- You and the law – the police
- You and the community – the school as a community
- You as a citizen – of the European Union
- You and the media – the power of advertising
- You and your opinions – speaking your mind
- You and your values – where do you stand?
- You and global issues – food and water
- You and the community – taking action on the local environment

Your Life 3
- You and the law – crimes and punishments (Citizenship 1a, 2a, 2b, 2c)
- You and the community – local government and local organisations (Citizenship 1c, 2a, 3b, 3c)
- You as a citizen – of the world (Citizenship 1g, 1i, 2a, 2b, 2c)
- You and the media – the power of the press (Citizenship 1h, 2a, 2b, 2c)
- You and your opinions – which political party do you support? (Citizenship 1d, 1e, 1f, 2a, 2b, 2c, 3a)
- You and your values – human rights issues (Citizenship 1a, 1f, 1i, 2a, 2b, 2c, 3a)
- You and global issues – poverty (Citizenship 1f, 1i, 2a, 2b, 2c, 3a)
- You and the community – pressure groups and campaigning (Citizenship 1f, 1h, 2a, 2b, 2c, 3b, 3c)

1 You and your body –

Your identity and image

Your teenage years are a period of rapid growth and change known as **adolescence**, during which you develop from a child into an adult. Your body changes and you develop sexually as you pass through puberty. Your character also changes. You become more independent, developing a greater sense of your identity and your own views, values and beliefs.

You and your identity

An important aspect of your identity is your personality – the features of your character that make you the sort of person you are.

What type of person are you? Do you see yourself as quiet and reserved or lively and outgoing? Are you happy-go-lucky or are you serious? Are you anxious or carefree? Do you enjoy being with other people or do you prefer being on your own?

Thinking about questions like these can help you to discover what sort of personality you have and to establish your identity.

Your values and beliefs

Some teenagers find that what they think conflicts with the views of the adults around them. You have to learn to make your own judgements, after considering different points of view.

When it comes to friendships, you may have some difficult choices to make. Of course, it's quite possible to be friends with someone who has different opinions from you, but what happens if you have totally different values? You may have to ask yourself: which matter more to me, my friendships or my values?

In groups

What characteristics would your ideal person have? On your own study the list of characteristics below. Rank them in order of importance, starting with 1 (the most important). Then form groups and discuss your lists.

> humble loyal confident gentle practical reliable intelligent generous artistic honest considerate hard-working sociable attractive witty athletic wealthy exciting forgiving tough

Your goals and ambitions

During adolescence, you may start to think about what you want to do with your life and what you hope to achieve. At first you may have no firm ideas about what you want to do. This may only become clear to you over a number of years, and you may change your mind many times before making a decision. Nevertheless, thinking about what you hope to achieve can be a useful way of developing your sense of identity.

In ten years' time

Here's what some people said when they were asked to think about what they'd like to have achieved in ten years' time:

'I'd like to have travelled and seen the world.'
'I want to be rich and famous.'
'I'd like to have got a university degree and found an interesting job.'
'I want to have had a good time. After all, you're only young once.'
'I'd like to have done something to help other people who are less fortunate than us.'

for your file

Write about how you see yourself in ten years' time and what you hope to have achieved by then.

adolescence

You and your image

As you develop into an adult you have to choose what image of yourself you want to give others. The impression you create depends chiefly on two things – the way you behave and the way you look.

There are lots of pressures on teenagers to make them dress or behave in certain ways – from parents, teachers and other teenagers; and from advertisers, television, newspapers and magazines. When you are deciding how you're going to behave and how you want to look, you need to be aware of these pressures.

In groups

Discuss the advice Jane Goldman gives (below) about the importance of being yourself and dressing the way you want to. Do you agree that 'most people want friends who are happy, balanced and behave normally'?

Discuss the advice she gives about how to cope with fashion. Do you agree that 'real friends don't care what you wear'? How important do you think it is to be fashion-conscious and to dress fashionably?

Give the right **impression** – Be yourself
by Jane Goldman

Are you **loud** or **boastful**?

Showing off, making incessant jokes and generally doing things that demand attention rarely wins any friends. It not only gives the impression that you're desperate, but it's also unattractive behaviour, and likely to put people off wanting to get to know you better. Being yourself is always the best bet.

Are you **ultra-nice**?

Being friendly wins points, but being crawly is the kiss of death. If you constantly agree with things people say, regularly compliment them on their clothes, talents etc, you are being crawly and it's very off-putting. Most people want friends who are happy, balanced and behave normally.

Do you **dress differently** from others?

Sadly, many young people are very freaked-out by others who don't conform. Whether it's because of your religion, because you're not into fashion, or simply because you like to be individual, just the fact that you stand out can put people off you. However, you should never need to change the way you look to suit others – just make an extra effort to get talking to people, show them that you like *them* the way *they* are, and once they've got to know your personality, they'll be bound to forget all about how you look.

Four ways to cope with fashion

1. If something comes into fashion, it's never worth pestering for it or breaking your piggy bank right away unless you truly adore it and could imagine yourself wearing it even *after* it went out of fashion. Wait a few weeks, and if you still want it, then it's probably worth it.

2. If there's no chance of getting anything new for a while, but you feel like your clothes are hideously out of date, your best bet is to wear stuff that's either classic (like jeans and a sweatshirt) or totally off-beat, because it makes a positive statement that you're *aware* of fashion but have deliberately chosen not to follow it.

3. Never be afraid to avoid a fad you're not that crazy about, even if all your friends are doing it. Real friends don't care what you wear.

4. Don't get too hung up about fashion – there really are far more important things in life. If your friends disagree with this statement, it's worth seriously considering getting some new, less shallow ones.

Adapted from Thirteen Something by Jane Goldman

You and your body – adolescence

Dealing with your feelings

Mood swings

Do you sometimes feel happy one minute and sad the next? These sudden changes of mood are a very normal part of growing up. Some of the problems might be caused by your hormones which are responsible for the physical changes you are going through.

You are changing from a child into a young adult, and new experiences are changing your view of the world. You may be excited and stimulated by what you discover. But you may also feel moody because you no longer enjoy the same things that you used to.

It's easy to blame the people around you for your state of mind. Perhaps you're feeling frustrated with your parents because they just don't seem to understand you any more. You may feel differently about your friends too. Some childhood friends now seem juvenile and annoying. Your mood can swing from wildly happy to desperately sad and back again.

Someone to talk to

Have you heard the saying 'a problem shared is a problem halved'? If you keep your problems to yourself they can seem a great deal worse than they really are. If you talk to somebody about your problem, you can come to see it in a different light. Maybe it's just arranging an emotion into words and then saying it out loud which does this. Sometimes you will find that the person you talk to can convince you that there is really nothing to worry about at all.

Different people can help you with different problems, so if you want to share a worry, decide who would be the best person to talk to about it.

From Growing Up

In groups

Study the list of problems (below) and decide which of these people you think it would be best to consult about that particular problem: **a)** best friend, **b)** parent, **c)** elder sister/brother, **d)** teacher, **e)** agony aunt, **f)** doctor, **g)** religious leader, **h)** social worker, **i)** confidential adviser, for example Childline.

1. Worries about your physical development or a sexual problem.
2. Constant arguments with your parents.
3. An emotional problem related to your boyfriend/girlfriend.
4. Unhappiness because you are being teased or bullied.
5. A problem because you have got involved in something illegal.
6. Loneliness because you don't seem able to make or keep friends.

Difficult feelings – Anger

'I get so angry all the time. My mum says I've got a problem and that I have to learn to calm down. But no matter how hard I try, something happens and I explode.' Cara

Anger is one of the primary emotions and despite its reputation it isn't a bad emotion. Like joy, pain and happiness, anger is a natural response to certain events. And just as expressing your happiness makes you feel good, it's better to express your anger rather than bottle it up where it ferments into nastiness.

Okay, so we all agree that it's good to express your anger, the trouble comes when you act on your anger by taking it out on others or yourself. People who say 'I couldn't help it, I was angry' made a choice to act out their anger. If this sounds like you, then it may help to look at exactly why you lash out and what you hope to achieve when you do. Rather than hit out or have a door-slamming session (which in the end, only leads to further trouble and greater loss of self-respect), walk away, count to ten, have a quiet think, and work out an assertive plan of action.

From Wise Guides: Self Esteem by Anita Naik

Coping with your moods

Although you can't avoid bad moods altogether, there are ways of controlling them. First of all, don't blame yourself for being moody. Try and think back over the hours until you hit on the moment things went wrong. The reason behind your mood swing may surprise you.

For example, one afternoon somebody takes your seat on the school bus. This makes you angry and upset, although it's nothing very serious. Your friends think you're silly for getting upset about it and when you think about it seriously afterwards, you will probably admit that losing your seat wasn't the real problem at all. Perhaps it simply triggered off all kinds of other thoughts about yourself. You think it shows that nobody likes you, or that you take people for granted. It's really these feelings that are at the core of your reaction.

Think positive

Finding the reason behind your bad moods should help you do something about them. Learn to recognize moods and control them, or they might start controlling you. Positive action of some kind will make you feel better.

If you feel moody, go for a walk and take a little time to be by yourself. When you've thought things over, you may be ready to talk to somebody. Some people find physical activity helps a bad mood. Offer to dig the garden or wash the car. Take your aggression out on something inanimate. Doing something quite simple and mindless for a while may make all the difference.

If there are certain people or situations that put you into a bad mood, try to avoid them. It is worth telling people how you feel and that you would rather be left alone. There's nothing worse than people who try to make you have a good time when you don't feel like it.

From Growing Up

⊕ In groups

Discuss what you have learned from these two pages about **a)** mood swings and how to cope with them, and **b)** how to deal with anger and frustration. Which pieces of advice do you think are the most useful?

for your file

Dear Dave
I'm finding life hard at present. Some days I feel great and everything's fine, other days I'm really down and people get on to me for being moody. Is there anything I can do to stop myself feeling like this?
Aston (14)

Write Dave's reply to Aston.

Difficult feelings – Frustration

'Sometimes I feel so frustrated that I could scream. I feel like I'm trapped and that no-one can hear what I'm saying.' Lena

Feeling frustrated comes from being misunderstood, ignored, or from being unable to achieve desired goals. Often a sense of frustration comes about because we don't really know what our goals are, so we thrash about trying different things only to find we're still not satisfied.

To give frustration its marching orders you have to accept that long-term happiness comes from within, and not from boyfriends, new clothes, make-up, careers, money or from going out. If you work at getting to know yourself (and liking what you find), then you won't look elsewhere for happiness.

From Wise Guides: Self Esteem by Anita Naik

2 You and your responsibilities –

Racism and racists

What is racism?

➔ **Racism** is the belief that people from some races are innately inferior to others, because of things like the colour of their skin, their ethnic origin, or the country they come from.

➔ **Prejudice** is knowing next to nothing about people but prejudging them anyway on the basis of stereotypes.

➔ **Racial discrimination** occurs when someone is treated less favourably because of their skin colour, or their racial, national or ethnic origin. Racial discrimination includes racial abuse and harassment and is against the law.

From *What is Racism?*, Commission for Racial Equality

In pairs

What is the difference between racism, prejudice and racial discrimination?

Racism is...

Five teenagers explain what racism means to them.

Having to keep relationships secret
" I can't walk down the street with my boyfriend because our families wouldn't approve of us going out together. "
Lisa, 15

Being ignored
" I'm Jewish so I didn't have to sing the hymns at assembly. I thought that was reasonable until the other girls at school started to ignore me because one said I thought I was something special. " Hannah, 13

Being singled out
" I was in McDonald's and these lads said to my friend, 'Why are you going round with a Paki?' and pointed at me. Then they made jokes about there being a smell of curry. "
Parveen, 17

Ignorance at home
" My mum says she doesn't mind me having black friends, but she would draw the line at me going out with 'one of them'. " Karl, 15

Not getting the respect you deserve
" I hate the way people talk to me as though I can't speak English, just because my parents are Chinese. They own a take-away and you would not believe the abuse they have to endure. " Anna, 18

From *Mizz*, issue 295 © Mizz/IPC Syndication

In groups

1 Discuss what the five teenagers (above) say racism means to them and how it affects them. Talk about what racism means to you.

2 'Racist jokes such as the ones made to Parveen aren't funny. As well as being insulting, they demean the person who tells them.' Discuss this view.

racism, prejudice and discrimination

Why are some people racist?

Racism has been defined as the belief that some of the 'races of mankind' are superior to others. The 'superior races' were seen as more intelligent, more civilised, more capable of scientific invention, and even more moral – in other words, better human beings. People have used this idea of 'higher races' and 'lower races' to justify slavery, forced transportation, economic exploitation and even genocide – the killing of hundreds of thousands of men, women and children because they were said to be members of certain 'races' and should be 'eliminated'.

Not only has this cruelty inflicted untold human suffering over the centuries, the very thing it has been based on – the idea that there are different races in the sense of types or grades – is now known by genetic science to be untrue. There are no such things as distinct races of mankind. Within the human form the range of differences is very large indeed, and the clustering of features such as skin colour and hair type – which are often taken to be the signs of racial difference – are juts a tiny part of the possible range of DNA variation of which we are made up. People with similar skin colour, for example, and alike in that way, are also unalike in so many other ways that to say they are members of a distinct 'race' makes little more sense than to say that people who can roll their tongues longways, and those who can't, are two distinct 'races'!

From *Racism* by Jagdish Gundara and Roger Hewitt

Racists – what's their problem?

Present-day racists hold their views for a number of different reasons …

Insecurity: Racists might not feel very good about themselves, so by bullying others they can forget their problems.

Upbringing: Many have racist views because their parents hold the same beliefs.

Bad experiences: Perhaps they've been in a situation before that has made them dislike an individual from a certain racial group. They may now hate people from the same background.

Fear of the unknown: Racists don't understand the groups they despise and have no interest in learning about other cultures or nationalities.

Arrogance: They believe that if everyone had the same upbringing and opinions as them the world would be perfect.

Intolerance: Racists believe people of other colours or nationalities shouldn't be living here.

From *Mizz*, issue 295, © Mizz/IPC Syndication

⊕ In groups

1 Some people say, 'There is only one race – the human race.' What does this mean? Do you agree?
2 Discuss how the idea that there are superior races has been used in the past to justify slavery, the persecution of the Jews in Nazi Germany and the system of apartheid in South Africa. Talk about the human suffering that has resulted.

⊕ In groups

Discuss the reasons which are suggested on this page as to why people are racist. Can you think of any other reasons? What do you think is the main reason?

You and your responsibilities – racism, prejudice and discrimination

Victims of racism

Four teenagers explain what it feels like to be the victims of racism.

'Don't they have any feelings?'
❝ Things are bad for my whole family at the moment. There's not one of us who hasn't had a problem, mum and dad included. We're not the only Bengali family in our area, but we seem to get most of the abuse from neighbours. They have no respect and put rubbish through our letter box and smash bottles outside the front door. When my sister got married we went to the cars and a gang of lads who hang around the flats started to shout abuse – on her wedding day. Don't they have any feelings? We have reported things but we don't have any proof of who is harassing us. I'm determined these people will be punished one day with the help of the authorities. ❞ Mila, 15, East London

'Can't they see more than my colour?'
❝ My mum is from the Philippines and my dad's English. But people are not interested in that and show their ignorance by calling me 'Chinky' at school, and going on about slanting eyes. I wish everyone was like my mum and dad. They love each other even though they come from totally different backgrounds and cultures. ❞ Tony, 14, Edinburgh

'I thought they were my friends'
❝ Our families have never had a problem with me and Jason going out together, but we've had a bit of hassle from people we'd been hanging around with.

We met in a nightclub and when we started seeing each other a few of my 'friends' made comments about me being better off going out with a white bloke. Jason's also had people saying they can't understand why he'd want to go out with a white girl, so the problems have come from both sides.

I started to get abusive phone calls at one point, so I got the police involved. They traced the calls to a girl who I used to think of as a good friend. I couldn't believe it – we'd been to a school where there were all religions and cultures, and had grown up with people of all races. I could never have thought of her as racist. ❞ Melissa, 17, West London

'Racism makes me determined to do well'
❝ I wanted a Saturday job so a friend got me an interview at the chemist's where she worked. But the manager was really off with me and I got a call almost straight away to say the job had gone to someone else. But I know the girl who got it and she didn't have an interview until after I got the call. I can't think there was any reason other than the fact I am black – I was better qualified than the other girl, who'd never worked in a shop before. It really hurts when you encounter that sort of thing but it makes me angry and more determined to be a success. ❞ Carol, 16, Birmingham

Adapted from Mizz, *issue 295, © Mizz/IPC Syndication*

Stephen Lawrence was 18 when he was set upon by a gang of youths and fatally stabbed in Eltham, South London, in April 1993. He died only yards from where a 16-year-old Asian youth, Rohit Duggal, had been murdered in a racial attack the previous year.

✚ In groups
Discuss what you learn from the stories on this page about what it feels like to be a victim of racism.

🔄 Role-play
In pairs, imagine that one of you has been the victim of racial harassment or racial abuse. Act out a scene in which they tell a friend what happened and how they felt during the incident and afterwards. Do the scene twice, taking it in turns to be the person who has been the victim of racism.

How great a problem is racism?

How much discrimination is there?

Racism can make it harder for people to get jobs, or take away people's jobs; it can mean they have poorer housing, or that they leave school or college with fewer qualifications; it can result in violent attacks, or it can lead to harsh treatment by the police or other authorities.

Most racial discrimination that takes place in Britain today is based on 'colour' and is directed against 'visible' minorities – for example, people of Asian, African, Caribbean and Chinese descent.

It is sometimes said that claims of racial discrimination are exaggerated, and that organisations like the Commission for Racial Equality only make matters worse. The fact is that while life has improved in many ways for ethnic minorities in Britain since the early 1950s, racial discrimination and harassment are still too often daily experiences for many people.

➡ The unemployment rate among people from ethnic minorities is more than twice the rate among white people.

➡ On average, pay rates for people from ethnic minorities are 10% less than for white people.

➡ The proportion of ethnic minority families who are homeless is three times as high as the proportion of white families who are homeless.

➡ The Home Office has accepted that there may be as many as 130,000 racially motivated incidents a year.

From *What is Racism?*, Commission for Racial Equality

✣ In groups

What is racial discrimination? Which groups of people are the main victims of racial discrimination? How serious a problem do you think racial discrimination is in Britain today?

Racism 'rife in justice system'

Every key stage of the criminal justice system is riddled with racism, leaving black people with a greater prospect of being arrested and jailed than whites, according to a study by a penal reform group.

British Afro-Caribbean people are seven times more likely to be in jail despite being no more likely to commit crimes, says the Howard League.

The report suggests that the unequal treatment suffered by black people at the hands of the police, identified by the Macpherson Report,* is practised by all parts of the criminal justice system.

The study shows that discrimination occurs despite people in ethnic minorities being in greatest need of protection by the criminal justice system as they are more likely to be victims of crime. Data from the British Crime Survey shows that Pakistanis and Bangladeshis are worst affected.

Frances Crook, director of the Howard League, said: 'The number of black people in our prisons is out of all proportion to the size of the black community, yet there is no evidence to suggest that people from ethnic minority groups commit more crime.

'The reasons for this are complex. It is partly a matter of social deprivation. But it is also clear that discrimination exists at every stage in the criminal justice system, from the chances of being arrested to the decision of the court and the length of the sentence.'

From *The Guardian*, 20 March 2000

* The report of an enquiry into the police handling of the investigation into the murder of Stephen Lawrence, known as the Macpherson Report, stated that police incompetence and institutional racism had hindered the search for Stephen's killers, who have never been brought to justice. The report also warned about complacency in other institutions.

What is institutional racism?

❝ *The collective failure of an organisation to provide an appropriate and professional service to people because of their colour, culture or ethnic origin.* ❞ – The Macpherson Report

❝ *Institutional racism is about stereotyping; it is about being unwitting; it is about ignorance; it is about failing to recognise a racist/hate crime; it is about not listening or understanding and not being interested in listening or understanding; it is about white pretence and black people being seen as a problem.* ❞ – John Grieve, director of the Metropolitan Police's Racial Task Force

✣ In groups

Discuss what is meant by institutional racism and what its effects can be.

You and your responsibilities – racism, prejudice and discrimination

Racism and the law

RACIAL ATTACKS AND HARASSMENT

If someone abuses or threatens you or damages your property because of your colour, race, nationality or ethnic origin that is **racial harassment**.

If someone uses any kind of physical violence against you because of your colour, race, nationality or ethnic origin that is **racial attack**.

Any of the following incidents are classified as a racial attack or harassment:

* personal attacks of any kind
* written or verbal threats or insults
* damage to property
* graffiti.

The sort of cases in which the police are most likely to initiate the prosecution process are:

* Acts intended or likely to stir up racial hatred (including the display and distribution of written material).
* Cases of assault, even those which appear to be minor, so long as the victim is prepared to give evidence that some harm resulted. Pain, injury or even psychological harm such as hysterical or nervous condition is enough in these cases.
* Threatening, abusive or insulting behaviour which is likely to cause alarm, harassment or distress to another.
* Damage to property such as broken windows, paint daubed on doors or walls, excrement pushed through letterboxes etc.

Such acts are totally unacceptable and are criminal offences.

From Racial Attacks and Harassment, The 1990 Trust

Racial discrimination and the law

The Race Relations Act (1976) made racial discrimination unlawful:

- in employment
- in education
- in the provision of goods and services, whether by individuals, businesses or local authorities
- in the sale, purchase and management of property.

The Act defined two types of discrimination – direct discrimination and indirect discrimination.

Direct discrimination occurs in a situation where a person is treated less favourably than another person would be on racial grounds.

Indirect discrimination occurs where there is a rule, policy, practice or condition that is applied to everyone equally but in practice leads to unequal treatment of people of one racial or ethnic group.

Although the Act prohibited both types of discrimination, indirect discrimination was outlawed only in limited respects in the public sector. Therefore, in 2000 Parliament introduced another Race Relations Act extending the law to make indirect discrimination unlawful throughout the public services in an effort to wipe out institutional racism. The police, prisons, schools, hospitals, councils and other public bodies cannot adopt policies which even unintentionally have the effect of discriminating against one section of the community.

⊕ In groups

Discuss the difference between direct discrimination and indirect discrimination. How has the law dealing with race relations been strengthened recently in order to prevent institutional racism?

TAKE A STAND AGAINST RACISM

If you think racism is wrong, you can do something about it.

The vast majority of people do not make racist remarks, and would never racially abuse anyone. But most of us can probably remember times when we witnessed racist behaviour and did nothing to stop it. Maybe it was an incident at work, or a comment overheard in the pub, or jokes and insults directed at other passengers on a bus or a train. It might even have come from a friend or relative, or a colleague, someone we respected. So we let it go. We didn't want to make a fuss. What difference would it make anyway?

The answer is: it can make all the difference.

By not speaking up you let others believe that their behaviour is acceptable. By speaking out, you can make them think about their words and actions. You may even stop them doing it again.

Sometimes all it takes is a few quiet words to persuade someone they are out of order.

If you see someone being harassed, or overhear someone making racist remarks – maybe in the canteen at work, or in the playground at school, or at a sports or leisure centre – tell someone such as a manager or teacher. They are responsible for doing something about it.

If someone is being racially abused or attacked in the street or another public place, you should report the incident directly to the police, without delay.

Be careful that you do not do anything that will put yourself or anyone else in danger. If you think a situation could get out of hand, get help as quickly as possible.

If you hear racist chanting at a football match, or another sports event, report it to the club or the appropriate sports authority.

If you see racist graffiti on a building, train or bus, complain to the owners and ask for it to be removed.

If you think a TV or radio programme, an advertisement or a newspaper article is insulting to people from a certain ethnic group, don't just shrug your shoulders – complain. Write to the editor, producer or company involved, and if you don't know their name, or aren't satisfied with their response, take it up with the relevant agency (e.g. the Press Complaints Commission).

It's up to all of us, whatever our colour or race, to make sure racist behaviour and attitudes are not accepted in Britain.

From Don't Shut Your Eyes, Commission for Racial Equality

What should I do?

❝ My older brother has started to go round with a racist gang. He's picking up their attitudes. How can I stop him from becoming a racist bully? ❞ Jan

❝ I've just started a new job. The other people there keeping making racist remarks about one of the girls because she's Asian. I'd like to do something about it, but I'm scared I'll antagonise them or that I'll even lose my job. What should I do? ❞ Sasha

❝ It's easy to know what you ought to do if you see a racist incident, but in practice it can be hard to do the right thing. ❞ Mike

❝ Reporting a racist incident in the playground is not telling tales, it's the responsible thing to do and the only way to stamp out racism. ❞ Jamila

In groups

1. Discuss what advice you would give to Jan and Sasha.
2. Discuss Mike and Jamila's views. Share any experiences you have had of witnessing racist incidents and say what action you took.

Role-play

In pairs, role play a scene involving two friends, one of whom quietly but firmly points out to the other that they are out of order because they've made a racist comment.

for your file

Write a letter to a newspaper saying why racism is unacceptable and why we must all make a stand against it.

3 You and your decisions –

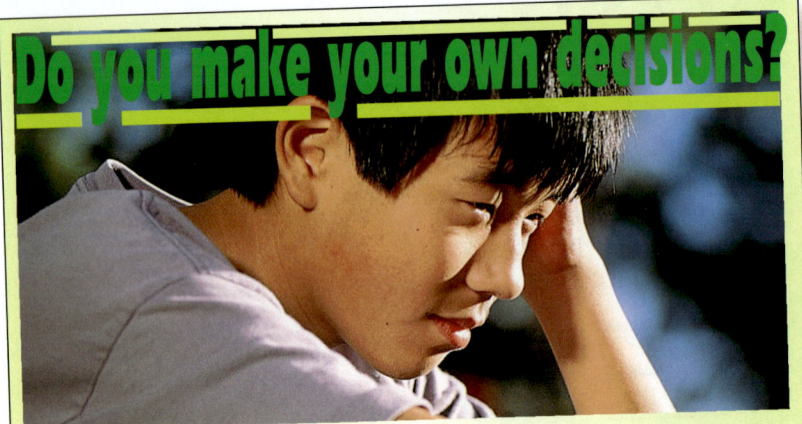

Do you make your own decisions?

How good are you at making up your own mind? Do you make your own decisions, or do you rely on other people, such as your parents, to help you? Do you wait to see what your friends are going to do before you commit yourself?

Answer this quiz to see how good you are at making your own decisions. Keep a record of your answers. Then check your score and discuss with a friend what you have learned about yourself from your answers.

1 Some kids in your street play jokes on an elderly person.
What do you do?
a Try to convince them it's a rotten thing to do.
b Ignore it: it's none of your business.
c Go along with them because they say it's OK.

2 Your parent says that your best friend in the whole world is a bad influence.
What do you do?
a Decide if he's a good friend, then give your parent a chance to get to know him better.
b Hang out with him behind your parent's back.
c Drop your friend because your parent says to.

3 You're not feeling very well, but your mates want you to go swimming.
What do you do?
a Decide if you're well enough, then give them your answer.
b Ask a parent to come up with an excuse.
c Go with them because they want you to.

4 The council want to build on the only green playing space near where you live.
What do you do?
a Decide if it's worth saving your play area, ask for more information and see what others in the neighbourhood think.
b Wait for someone else to do something about it.
c Nothing, because you don't care.

5 During an RE lesson you hear something that is different to what you and your family believe.
What do you do?
a Talk it over with the teacher and the class, then decide if you should mention it to your parents.
b Shrug it off – maybe somebody else will sort this one out.
c Go along with it.

What's your score?

All or mostly as:
You can make decisions for yourself and then act on them.

All or mostly bs:
You like sitting on the fence rather than making a decision. Only problem: fence sitting can be uncomfortable and you might fall off!

All or mostly cs:
You need to exercise your mind; you're not using it at all. Others are doing your thinking for you.

✚ In groups

What are the most important things to remember when you're making a decision?
- Honesty
- What your friends will think
- Respect for yourself and others
- Staying safe
- Tolerance
- Looking tough
- Fairness
- That you're right and everyone else is wrong.

Add to this list any other things you think are important, and rank them in order of importance. Then share your views in a class discussion.

Adapted from *Young Citizen ... Growing Up* by Kate Brookes

how to make decisions

Who influences you?

Study the chart (right). It shows the people who may play a part in your life. Which of them influences you the most? On a piece of paper write down *five* people who influence you. Put them in order, starting with the person who influences you the most.

Mother
Aunt(s)/Uncle(s)
Grandmother/Grandfather
Father
Headteacher
Elder sister/brother
YOU
Form tutor
Subject teacher(s)
Best friend
Other friends
Other adult(s) (e.g. youth leader, friend's mother, sports coach)

Why do they influence you?

That person influences me because she/he ...

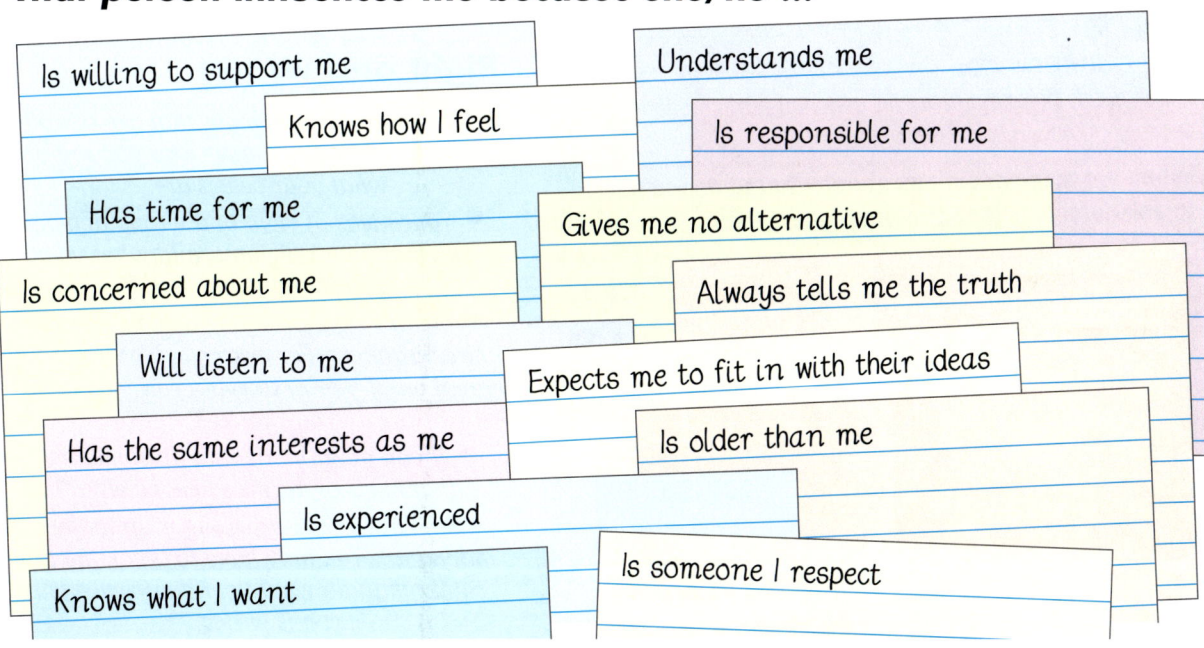

- Is willing to support me
- Understands me
- Knows how I feel
- Is responsible for me
- Has time for me
- Gives me no alternative
- Is concerned about me
- Always tells me the truth
- Will listen to me
- Expects me to fit in with their ideas
- Has the same interests as me
- Is older than me
- Is experienced
- Is someone I respect
- Knows what I want

In groups

1 Each go through the list of reasons (above). Beside the names of the five people who influence you, write down the reasons why that person influences you. (They may be different from the reasons given above.) Then, form groups and discuss who influences you and why.

2 List some of the important decisions a 14-year-old has to make. Talk about them one by one. Discuss whose advice you would listen to when making each decision.

for your file

Write about a time when you had a difficult decision to make and you asked people for their advice. Say whose opinion influenced you the most and why. Looking back, do you think you made the right decision?

You and your decisions – how to make decisions

Consider the consequences

When we try to work out what is the right or wrong thing to do, we often find that things aren't always straightforward. Sometimes it is easy to know what is the right or wrong thing to do; at other times it is not. As we grow up we begin to discover what is right and wrong. Some of the ways we discover these things are:

by consequence:
If I do such and such a thing, this is likely to happen.

by example:
Watching how other people behave and copying them.

by experience:
If you do something, you find out what happens. This will affect what you do in the future.

by following rules:
Many rules have been made to try to protect people.

by our feelings:
If somebody hurts me I may (or may not) hurt somebody else because I know what it feels like.

When we make decisions about what to do we have to ask ourselves the following questions:

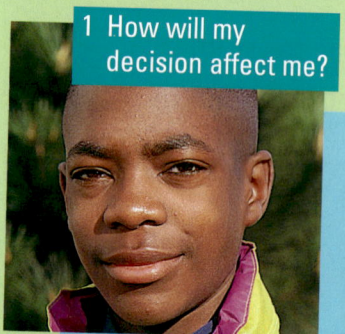

1 How will my decision affect me?

2 How will my decision affect my family and friends?

3 How will my decision affect my community?

4 How will my decision affect the world?

Long-term consequences: Tracey's story

Sometimes when somebody does something, the consequences of that action can stay with that person for the rest of their life. It is very important that we think about long-term consequences, because a wrong action or decision can ruin lives.

When Tracey was sixteen she got very drunk at a party. She ended up sleeping with an older man she didn't know. A few months later she began feeling ill and was diagnosed HIV positive.

From *Introducing Moral Issues* by Joe Jenkins

Right and wrong

❝ There are certain things that are morally right or wrong no matter who you are or what your beliefs are. ❞

❝ Your ideas of right and wrong depend on what your religion is and what your beliefs and values are. ❞

❝ What's right or wrong depends on the circumstances. For example, it's wrong to steal but if you're starving you may have no choice. ❞

❝ It can never be right to do something that hurts or harms someone else. ❞

❝ What's right or wrong is up to the individual. You may have to break the law rather than do what your conscience tells you is wrong. ❞

In groups

Discuss these ideas of right and wrong. Give reasons to support your views.

for your file

Write a statement for your folder in which you list examples of behaviour which you think is wrong, explaining why you think such behaviour is wrong.

Stay in control of your life

Don't let friends push you into doing something with them that you'd never dream of doing on your own. You owe it to yourself to make your own decisions rather than to allow others to make your decisions for you. It can be hard to say 'No' but not only will you respect yourself for doing so, other people will respect you too.

What is Peer Pressure?

What exactly is peer pressure? Well, it's when your friends try to encourage you to do something because they're doing it. Quite often it is something that is illegal or at least bound to cause strife. It's important to understand why your friends are so eager for you to join them; it's not because they want you to be the same, but because they don't want you to be different.

These are the areas in which peer pressure is exerted: having sexual relationships, drinking alcohol, smoking, drug-taking, shoplifting, skiving off school, lying, and driving without a licence.

Your friends might try to tempt you into these things by saying that you're a chicken if you don't. They may also give you the cold shoulder and threaten to spread nasty gossip unless you do what they want you to do. These guys will sink really low to make sure that you are in a position where you can't say no.

If you have a friend or a group of friends who are trying to force you to break the law, take drugs or do anything else that you don't really want to do, you need to ask yourself this: Are these people really my friends? The only honest answer is 'no'.

From *Friends or Enemies* by Anita Naik

What to do when making decisions

Use this 5-point plan whenever you are faced with making an important decision.

1. Find out all the **facts** you need to know. The more information you have, the easier it is to come to a wise decision.

2. Consider what the **alternatives** are. What are the different courses of action open to you?

3. Consider the **consequences** of each course of action. Ask other people what they think and listen to the reasons they give for their views.

4. Make up your own mind and **take action**. Take the decision which you think is right.

5. Having made the decision, **study the effects** of your decision. If things don't turn out as you expected, then be prepared to reconsider your decision after a while. But don't act too hastily and don't change your decision just because you encounter a difficulty.

You can use the letters in the word **FACTS** to help you to remember what to do when making decisions:

- Find out the **F**acts.
- Consider the **A**lternatives.
- Consider the **C**onsequences.
- Decide and **T**ake action.
- Review and **S**tudy the effects.

🔄 Role play

Discuss situations in which a person may have to make a tough decision because their friends are pressurising them to do something they do not want to do. Talk about different ways of dealing with the situation and role play a scene in which a young person stays in control and resists the pressure to do something they do not want to do.

4 You and your family –

Parents and teenagers

There are tensions and conflicts at times in all families. It's a part of family life. Part of becoming an adult is learning to understand what causes arguments between parents and teenagers and how to deal with them.

Top ten causes of tension between parents and teenagers
1. The state of your bedroom
2. The clothes you want to have and wear
3. The volume of the music you listen to
4. The people you choose as your friends
5. Your failure to do your share of household chores
6. The time you come in at night
7. The amount of time you spend watching TV
8. The language you use and the way you speak
9. The amount of time you spend on the phone
10. How much homework you do

In pairs

1. Discuss the things that cause conflicts between parents and teenagers. In your experience what are the top three issues that cause tension between them?
2. Do you think parents try to control teenagers' lives too much? How much independence do you think parents should give teenagers of your age?

How to deal with differences

One way that you can try to avoid conflict between parents and teenagers is to draw up and agree a list of ground rules. Here's the start of a list of ground rules that Dave (14) and his parents drew up:

> Dave's room – We agree that your room's your own and that we won't come in without knocking or asking your permission and that you will take responsibility for it, changing the sheets regularly and doing a big clean-up at least once a month. You agree that you'll not leave your things lying around the rest of the house and will help to keep it tidy.

Draft details of other ground rules that Dave might have drawn up, for example about homework, going out with his friends, using the phone, playing his music.

How to get on better

Here's what some people had to say when asked to suggest things that parents and teenagers could do in order to get on better.

> *Most parents are very supportive. The trouble is that they are so concerned that they are often over-protective. If only they'd let teenagers be more independent, they'd have fewer arguments and everyone would be less stressed.*

> *Teenagers can't just expect parents to trust them. They need to make an effort to show they can be trusted. Once their parents realise that they can be relied on to behave in a sensible manner, they'll find they lighten up.*

> *I think that communication between parents and teenagers is the crucial thing. If they spent more time together, for example by sitting down and having meals together and talking rather than watching TV, there'd be more understanding and less arguments.*

In groups

Discuss these viewpoints. Suggest other things that you think parents and teenagers could do to help them get on better.

becoming an adult

Arguments and How to survive them

Erica Stewart offers advice on what to do when you and your parents have a difference of opinion.

1. Keep calm. Shouting at them isn't going to get your views across. It's only likely to make the argument develop into a full-scale row.

2. Consider what's causing the disagreement. Is it a big deal that's worth having a major argument about? If it's not, then why not back down?

3. Say exactly how you feel and why you feel that way. Don't just make general accusations like 'You never let me do what I want.'

4. Stick to the point. Don't bring up past disputes. Concentrate on the issue at hand.

5. Listen to their point of view. Try to understand where they are coming from and whether they are genuinely concerned for your welfare.

6. Be prepared to compromise. Accepting a compromise shows that you are adult enough to understand that arguments occur because people have different viewpoints and that the way to resolve them is to find some middle ground.

7. Remember that you may not be in the right. For example, maybe your music was a bit loud and they've got a case for feeling annoyed.

8. Be prepared to say sorry. If you did lose it, storming off in a rage, then an apology is in order. It's hard to do, but it's the adult thing to do.

Educate your parents
by Philip Hodson

One thing I say is that children sometimes need to educate their parents. Educating your parents means showing them, by behaving in an adult way, that you are ready for a bit more freedom than they realised. They are only going to treat you in a grown-up way if you:

+ learn to negotiate
+ don't make angry demands
+ give them reasons for your viewpoint
+ show that you have researched the problem.

So when your dad is shouting at you (i.e. behaving like a child) because you want to go to the fair till 10.30 at night, show him that you have thought about how to get there safely, how to get back, how to pay for it and why a treat is due.

From *Letters to Growing Pains* by Philip Hodson

In pairs

Discuss the advice which Philip Hodson and Erica Stewart give on how to behave in an adult way. What do you think are the most useful pieces of advice?

Role play

Choose a situation in which a parent and teenager are clashing over what the parent sees as a piece of unacceptable behaviour by the teenager. Role play the scene twice – first showing the teenager reacting in a childish way, then showing the teenager behaving in a more adult way.

for your file

Write two versions of a story describing an argument between a teenager and one of their parents. (You could base it on a real-life incident.) In one version show the argument ending in a full-scale row. In the other version show it being resolved.

You and your family – becoming an adult

Rights and responsibilities

As you become an adult, you become aware of your **rights**. But it is important to realise that having rights also means having **responsibilities**.

My Bill of Rights

Everyone has rights, and though priorities may be different there are many 'expectations' that we hold in common. Some of these are included in the following list:
- I have a right to be treated well.
- I have a right to be listened to.
- I have a right to ask for something, even though I might not get it.
- I have a right to privacy.
- I have a right to make up my own mind.
- I have a right to be happy.
- I have a right to be different.

Adapted from Wise Guides: Self Esteem by Anita Naik

In groups

"*The best way to deal with a problem involving your brother or sister is to get your parents to help you deal with it.*"

"*It's better to deal with it yourself, but don't threaten them or try to bribe them. The way to get them to change their behaviour is to talk through the problem.*"

Discuss these views. What do you think is the best way to deal with a problem caused by your brother or sister? Should you try to deal with it yourself or is it better to get your parents involved too?

In pairs

1. On your own, copy out the 'Bill of Rights' and add any others that are important to you. List them in order of importance, then compare your list with a partner's.
2. Talk about how you feel when one of your rights is denied you. Discuss how important it is to respect other people's rights.

for your file

Make a copy of your bill of rights. Write this statement underneath your list: 'In return for these rights, I will respect the rights of others.'

Coping with brothers and sisters

Top ten causes of tension between brothers and sisters

1. Borrowing your things without asking permission
2. Failing to respect your privacy
3. Arguing over the use of either the computer or the TV
4. Disturbing you when you're busy
5. Saying embarrassing things or putting you down
6. Wanting you to play with them/help with their homework
7. Arguing about whose turn it is to do the chores
8. Getting in the way when you have friends around
9. Manipulating you by threatening to tell your parents something
10. Saying/doing things that they know irritate you and wind you up

Taking responsibility

Part of becoming an adult is learning to take responsibility within the family. Exactly what this involves will depend on your family circumstances, **says Fiona Johnson**.

FOR ELLA it meant looking after her two younger brothers, while her mum was recovering from a serious illness.

> I was only 12 at the time, but there was no one else who could do it. Our dad left years ago and we've no close relatives. My mum's friend came in when she could, but she's got a full-time job and because she's a manager she has to work long hours. Having to cope made me realise just how much mum did for us all. Now she's better I still help her much more than I ever did before she was ill.

FOR JASON it means calling in to see his grandad twice a week, just to check he's OK.

> Since gran died, grandad's been living on his own and finding it very difficult to cope. So mum used to call in and see him every day on her way home from work. We could all see it was getting her down. So I said I'd call in twice a week as those are the days I go to football practice and he lives near the park where we go. As a result I've got to know grandad and mum says it does him a power of good to see me. Sometimes I go round at weekends now to save her visiting then too.

FOR RAJ it means taking responsibility for walking the dog twice a day.

> My dad used to do it, but then he got promotion which means that he has to be out of the house by seven o'clock and he's often not back till late. So we had this family conference and it was quite clear that no one else could do it, so I said I'd be responsible for taking him out. Actually I quite enjoy it now – except when the weather's awful – and it's good exercise.

All these young people acted in an adult way because, in their different ways, they realised that they could do something which would help support the other people in their families. Being a teenager can be difficult. There are all sorts of pressures on you. But other members of your family have pressures on them. You can sometimes ease the pressures on other family members by taking responsibility and behaving in an adult way.

From *Taking Responsibility* by Fiona Johnson

Who's responsible?
by Derek Stuart

How much do you really do for yourself? Could you take more responsibility for the little things in life?

→ Who buys your toothpaste?
→ Who checks that your bike is safe to ride?
→ Who washes your games kit?
→ Who makes your packed lunch?

Teenagers often complain that their parents won't let them live their own lives. Then they complain when things aren't done for them.

If you answered 'I do' to all four questions at the beginning of the article, then maybe you really have begun to take responsibility for your own life. If not, then either stop whinging or do something about it.

From *Derek Says* by Derek Stuart

⊕ In groups

1 What do 'being responsible' and 'taking responsibility' mean?

2 Discuss what you learn from Fiona Johnson's article about young people taking responsibility within their families. Share experiences of times when you have taken responsibility for something within your families.

3 Talk about what Derek Stuart says in his article. Say why you agree or disagree with his view. Who do you think should be responsible for the 'little things in life' – you or someone else in your family?

5 You and your values –

What are human rights?

All people – whoever they are and wherever they live – have certain basic human rights.

We are entitled to more than just enough food, air and water in order to survive. Beyond these needs are basic human rights which underline our freedom; protecting us from abuse, illegal arrest, torture or execution.

Unfortunately, governments have a bad track record of preserving their citizens' human rights. This became clear when the full scale of Nazi crimes emerged at the end of the Second World War. Out of this grew the desire that it should never happen again. The result was the United Nations Organisation. It was hoped that the UN would provide a place where nations could go to resolve conflicts peacefully.

In 1948, the 48 members of the UN signed the Universal Declaration of Human Rights. It contained 30 separate articles describing the basic rights every person can expect, from fair pay to the right to a fair trial. A special United Nations Commission was also established to monitor countries for any signs of human rights' abuses. The UN also gave itself the muscle to implement economic sanctions on countries that were found guilty of human rights' abuse or to send in armed troops to protect civilians – particularly during wars.

Beyond the basics

Then in 1950 a special European Convention on Human Rights was passed by the 15 member-countries of an organisation called the Council of Europe. This created a Human Rights Court in Strasbourg, France. Now, if individuals or organisations in any of these European countries felt that their human rights had been violated by their government, they could ask for permission to bring their case to the Strasbourg court – where any decision made was binding on the home state.

Since 1950, UK governments have lost more than 50 cases in Strasbourg and have been found guilty of violating 11 of the 15 Convention rights.

Many people believe that Britain has a strong tradition of freedom and tolerance, but in fact its law never had a definite statement of its citizens' rights. This changed in October 2000 when the European Convention on Human Rights was adopted by the UK legal system.

One weakness of the UN Declaration was felt to be Article 26 (the rights of children). Because so many countries were ignoring it, a separate convention on the Rights of the Child was drawn up. Every country has signed up to it, except Somalia and America.

Adapted from 'Beyond the basics' by Jerome Monahan, *Guardian Education*, 11 April 2000

Violations of human rights

Since 1948, millions of people have been slaughtered by their governments for their origins, ideas or beliefs; in the killing fields of Indonesia and Rwanda, Iraq, Guatemala, Argentina, the former Yugoslavia, Cambodia and many other places. Millions more have been jailed in the prisons of states of every ideology from right to left, from Apartheid's jails in South Africa to Soviet *gulags* and Chinese *laogai*. Tens of millions of refugees have fled from oppression. Poverty, sickness and hunger have been the lot of much of the world's population. Each day of the week, every single one of the 30 Articles of the Declaration is being violated somewhere in the world.

Amnesty International

In groups

1 What do you think are the ten most basic human rights? Draw up a charter listing your top ten human rights, then compare your ideas with those of other groups.

2 Collect examples from newspapers and from the Internet of human rights violations around the world. Put them on display in your classroom.

human rights issues

Case study – Archana Guha

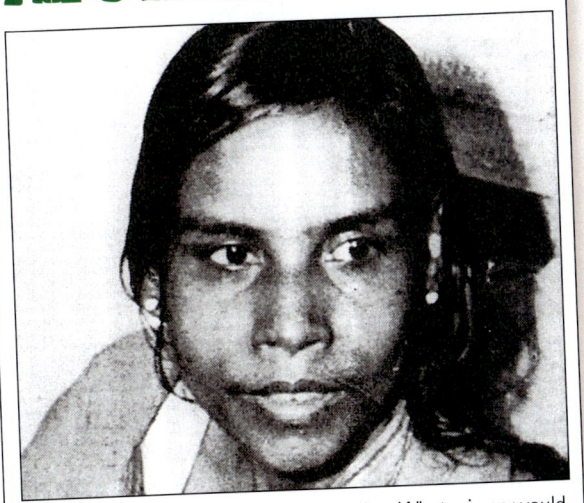

Imagine that you are arrested by the police. What crimes would you expect to be arrested for? Theft? Vandalism? Violence? All these are accepted crimes. How would you feel if you were arrested because your brother was suspected of committing a crime? That is what happened to Archana Guha, a primary school headmistress in India. She was 33 years old.

> The Universal Declaration of Human Rights states that 'No one shall be subject to arbitrary arrest, detention or exile.'

Assume that you have now been taken to the police station. How long would you expect to stay there without being charged with a crime? A few hours? Overnight perhaps?
Or three years? This is what happened to Archana Guha. She was 36 years old when she was finally released by the authorities.

> The Universal Declaration of Human Rights states that 'Everyone is entitled to a fair and public hearing by an independent and impartial tribunal.'

Imagine that the authorities are keeping you in prison. How would you expect to be treated? They will want to ask questions, and you will be kept in a cell. Would you expect to have your feet and hands tied, and to be hung from a pole? Your feet beaten? Your hips kicked? Cigarette burns on your feet? Your family threatened unless you cooperate? This is what happened to Archana Guha. She was paralysed when she finally left prison.

> The Universal Declaration of Human Rights states that 'No one shall be subjected to torture or to cruel, inhuman or degrading treatment or punishment.'

Assume that you suffered such imprisonment and torture without trial. What would you expect to happen when you managed to tell the authorities? An investigation? The trial of the guilty policemen? Compensation paid to you? And when would you expect some action on your case? A few months, perhaps. Maybe a year or so before the case is brought to court. But Archana had to wait 22 years. By this time, three of the policemen involved had died, one had been promoted, and one had retired.

> The Universal Declaration of Human Rights states that 'All are entitled to equal protection of the law.'

Assume you have gone through the agonies of physical and mental abuse that Archana Guha has. What punishment would you expect the policemen to receive? A long prison sentence? Perhaps as long as the one you went through? Perhaps longer? How would you feel if they only received about one year's imprisonment and a fine of $60? This is what happened to Archana Guha. She was 55 years old when the case was finally concluded.

> The Universal Declaration of Human Rights states that 'Everyone has the right to an effective remedy for acts violating fundamental rights granted by law.'

The case of Archana Guha is not unique. There are thousands of people around the world imprisoned without charge, tortured by the state, and left physically and mentally scarred. There are thousands of cases where the authorities who have carried out the human rights abuses are still working, some have been promoted, others have gone into peaceful retirement. But justice has not caught up with them.

Adapted from Human Rights Assembly Pack, Amnesty International UK

Can torture ever be justified?

Some people argue that in certain circumstances torture can be defended as a 'necessary evil'. In the case of terrorists or enemy agents, they say, torture can be justified because it is a way of getting information quickly and, perhaps, saving innocent people from suffering as a result. Others argue that torture is inhumane and morally wrong and that the pain and suffering of the victim cannot be justified.

⊕ In groups

What do you think about the morality of torture? Organise a debate on the motion 'This house believes that there are no circumstances in which the use of torture can be justified.'

25

You and your values – human rights issues

Freedom of thought

'Everyone has the right to freedom of thought, conscience and religion.'

You have the right to hold views on any issue you like without fear of punishment or censure. You also have the right to believe in any religion – or none at all. You have the right to change your religion if you wish, and to practise and teach your religion or beliefs.

Article 18 of the Universal Declaration of Human Rights

Suffering for your beliefs

From the Christian crusades to the shooting of supporters of democracy in Tiananmen Square, China, people have suffered for what they believe in. In Saudi Arabia, Christian church services are not allowed. In Northern Ireland, Catholics and Protestants have been killed because of their religion. When will this end?

Would you be prepared to go to prison for your religion?

That's what a Tibetan nun, Ngawang Sangdrol, did in August 1990, when she was only 13 years old. She and other Buddhist nuns from the Guru monastery went on a demonstration against the ruling Chinese government, calling for Tibetan independence. Ngawang was arrested and even though, at 13, she was too young to be tried, she was held prisoner for nine months.

On her release, Ngawang was forbidden to rejoin her monastery, but this didn't stop her from doing it. She was arrested again in 1992 for demonstrating, and sentenced to three years' imprisonment. Whilst in prison, Ngawang and twelve other Buddhist nuns made secret tapes of uplifting Tibetan protest songs. She was given a further six years in prison.

From Stand up for Your Rights, Peace Child International

⊕ In groups

" *I admire Ngawang for sticking up for her beliefs and principles, but I wouldn't be prepared to sacrifice my freedom as she has done.* "

" *If I were in Ngawang's position, I'd be prepared to do what she did.* "

Discuss these views and say whether or not you'd be prepared to go to prison for your beliefs.

Conscientious objectors

A **pacifist** is a person who believes that any kind of violence is unjustifiable and that you should not participate in war or be a member of any armed force.

Because pacifists believe that all forms of fighting are morally wrong, they will refuse to join the army when they are called up for national service. A person whose conscience will not allow them to fight is known as a **conscientious objector**.

Conscientious objectors are often made to suffer for their beliefs. In addition to being branded cowards, they may be tried and imprisoned. During the First World War, some conscientious objectors were shot for refusing to fight.

In countries where all young people are expected to do a period of national service, a conscientious objector may be sent to prison. That's what happened to Savvas Enotiadis, a 24-year-old Greek, whose religious beliefs made him refuse to serve in the armed forces. When he said that his religious beliefs made it impossible for him to agree to do military service, he was given a four-year prison sentence.

⊕ In groups

" *It is everyone's duty to fight to defend their country if they are called upon to do so.* "

" *People who have moral objections to fighting should not be punished for their beliefs.* "

" *It takes more courage to be a conscientious objector than it does to join up and go and fight.* "

Discuss these views. What is your view of people who are pacifists? Should they be allowed to refuse to serve in the armed forces? Should they be imprisoned if they refuse to do so? Would you be prepared to do military service if you were to be conscripted?

Freedom of expression

> 'Everyone has the right to freedom of opinion and expression.'
>
> You have the right to tell people your opinion. You should be able to express your views, however unpopular, without fear of punishment. You have the right to communicate your views within your country and to people in other countries.
>
> *Article 19 of the Universal Declaration of Human Rights*

Jailed for Joking

Q: When is a joke not a joke?
A: When it lands you in prison.

In 1990 in Myanmar (Burma) there was a general election which was won by the National League for Democracy (NLD). The military government chose to ignore the election results and instead placed the NLD leader, Daw Aung San Suu Kyi (pronounced Ong San Soo She), under house arrest.

In January 1996, two comedians – U Pa Pa Lay and U Lu Zaw – performed in Daw Aung San Suu Kyi's home. They sang comic songs about the country's generals and told jokes about repression by the military rulers. They had every right to make their jokes under Articles 18 and 19 of the Universal Declaration of Human Rights, which guarantee freedom of thought and freedom of expression. But their rights were blatantly violated when both men were sentenced to seven years in prison in March 1996.

'My moustache and I were in jail for one year and eight months ... all because of making jokes.'
U Pa Pa Lay referring to his imprisonment in the 1990s.

From The Universal Declaration of Human Rights

Amnesty International

Amnesty International is a worldwide movement which campaigns for human rights. It is independent of any government, political faction, ideology, economic interest or religion. Its aims are:

- to seek the release of all prisoners of conscience as long as they have not used or encouraged violence;
- to ask fair and prompt trials for all political prisoners;
- to campaign for the abolition of the death penalty and of torture and all forms of cruel, inhuman or degrading treatment or punishment.

It targets individual cases, such as U Pa Pa Lay's, through letter-writing campaigns – getting members to write letters to the authorities appealing for prisoners to be either released or given a fair trial.

There are hundreds of Amnesty Youth Action Groups in schools, colleges and youth clubs in the UK, which campaign for human rights, in addition to over 200 Junior Urgent Action letter-writing groups.

For information:
e-mail: student@amnesty.org.uk
website: www.amnesty.org.uk
address: Youth and Student Office, Amnesty International UK, 99–119 Rosebery Avenue, London EC1R 4RE

In groups

1 Discuss what freedom of expression means.
2 Does freedom of expression mean that you can say or publish what you want? What do you feel about people who put pornography or racist literature on the internet? Should they be allowed to do this or should they be banned? What types of material, if any, should be banned?

for your file

How important is the right to freedom of expression? Write a short statement giving your views.

You and your values – human rights issues

The rights of women

Women's rights in the UK

Sexual discrimination is unlawful under the Sex Discrimination Acts of 1975 and 1986. These Acts make it illegal to treat anyone less favourably, on the grounds of their sex, than a person of the opposite sex is treated in the same circumstances. Sex discrimination is not allowed in employment, education, the provision of goods, facilities and services and in advertising.

Discrimination at work

The Sex Discrimination Acts have done much to ensure that women are no longer discriminated against by employers in terms of recruitment. Women have equal rights to enter most occupations. However, in a number of ways women are still losing out to men in the world of work.

A much higher percentage of women than men are in low-paid jobs. For example, over 90 per cent of domestic staff and secretaries are women. Similarly, less than 10 per cent of surgeons and electrical engineers are women.

Although Article 23 of the Universal Declaration of Human Rights states that 'Everyone has the right to equal pay for equal work', women's earnings still lag behind men's earnings for both manual and non-manual workers.

While the number of women managers continues to increase, there are still more male managers than female managers. Also, attitudes are slow to change. A research project for the Pitman group in 1998 showed that over 80 per cent of employees (both men and women) still preferred a man to be the boss.

> 'Everyone is entitled to the same human rights.'
>
> You should not suffer discrimination, or be deprived of your rights, because of your race, colour, sex, language, religion, sexual orientation or political opinions.'
>
> *Article 2 of the Universal Declaration of Human Rights*

The Right to Fight

IN Britain, women in the armed forces are non-combative but can support frontline roles. The government retains the right to exclude women soldiers from units, such as the Royal Marines, likely to be involved in 'close and kill' actions. Women are not allowed on submarines because of the risk to foetuses from recycled air. Overall, 70% of positions in the army, 76% in the navy and 96% in the RAF are open to women. Women make up 6.5% of the forces.

From The Guardian, 12 January 2000

In groups

1 Discuss the view that all positions in the armed forces should be open to women.

2 Why do you think there are still more men than women in high-paid jobs?

Women's rights around the world

The twentieth century saw a huge advance in the status of women in many countries. However, in some parts of the world discrimination against women continues.

But more and more women are beginning to stand up for their rights, even in strict Islamic countries such as Iran.

for your file

Study the article 'Iran's female students protest at segregation' and write an editorial for a newspaper either supporting or condemning the students' actions.

Iran's female students protest at segregation
Medical school sit-ins reflect growing demands for sexual equality

IN a daring challenge to the Islamic system, female medical students in Iran are refusing to attend classes and are staging sit-ins in protest at their segregation from men in universities. The students believe they receive an inferior medical education to their male peers.

One medical school in the holy Shi'ite city of Qom is for women only, and in Tehran's universities men and women must attend classes in separate rooms or sit on opposite sides of the classroom.

'We suffer because we have little interaction with our male classmates. We rarely have an exchange of ideas. There is a wall between us,' said Homa, 24, a student at Tehran university's medical school.

This week a group of female medical students called upon President Mohammed Khatami and the country's supreme leader, Ayatollah Ali Khamenei, to reverse what they believe is sex discrimination. They have also complained to the health ministry.

Such action may not guarantee immediate change. But their public dissent adds a significant voice to a growing demand for sexual equality.

There is growing opposition to the inequality between the sexes that continues despite the significant gains women have made since the 1979 Islamic revolution.

Today, there are more women than men in higher education and women are increasingly seen in important positions of authority.

Women were encouraged to attend medical school after the revolution so they could treat female patients, in line with conservative readings of Islamic teachings. But these opportunities no longer satisfy women in modern Iran.

'In theory, our government says women are equal. But in practice and in our culture this is not the case,' said one woman, a 25-year-old medical student.

From *The Guardian*, 29 January 2000

VIOLENCE AGAINST WOMEN

Violence against women, in the home and outside it, is a global phenomenon. Worldwide, more than 20% of women experience some degree of domestic violence during marriage.

- In a survey of 796 Japanese women, 77% reported that they had experienced some form of domestic battery.
- In South Africa, the Women's Bureau estimates that one in four women is beaten by her male partner.
- In the US a woman is beaten every 15 seconds.
- In Britain, more than 25% of violent crimes reported to the police are domestic violence of men against women, making it the second most violent crime.

But …
- 44 countries have passed laws against domestic violence.
- 17 countries have made marital rape a crime.
- 27 countries have passed sexual harassment laws.

Adapted from *New Internationalist*, January–February 1998

In groups

1 'Hitting your partner can never be justified, no matter what they have done.' Discuss this view.

2 How would you define sexual harassment? Make a list of all the different types of behaviour which you think are examples of sexual harassment.

What do you think should happen to someone who is found guilty of sexually harassing a person **a)** at work, **b)** in public?

6. You and your feelings – dealing with loss

Coping with grief

How you may feel after a death

Shock
You will nearly always feel shock after a member of your family or a close friend has died. Even though the person may have died after a long and serious illness it can still be a shock – all the more so if they died suddenly, in an accident, for instance. Part of being in shock is disbelief – you may not believe that this is happening to you. You may find that you are somehow denying that it is really happening at all. 'It can't be', 'This isn't true' – these are the sorts of things that you may think or say. You will probably feel numb at times, as if you are not feeling anything at all. Many people react this way immediately after a death. Being in shock and 'denial' is a natural way of protecting us from being overwhelmed by too many painful feelings.

Sadness
Once the reality of the death has seeped in, you will probably feel a terrible sense of sadness, loss and loneliness. You may be very unhappy indeed, especially in the early days, and you may want to cry a lot. This sadness is one of the strongest feelings that you may have after someone dies. It is an important part of grieving, and not something to be bottled up (see page 31). However, the extremes of sadness should lessen gradually as time goes on.

Anger
You might feel angry as well – above all, angry with the person who has died for leaving you. This is perfectly natural, but anger is one of the most difficult feelings to admit to, even to yourself. That is why your anger may be directed towards others, for example doctors and nurses, the priest, other adults for not telling you in time that the person was dying – even at life itself for being so unfair. Anger is a common response to the pain of bereavement. It only becomes harmful if you begin to feel it all the time, or if you always turn it against yourself in a punishing way. You should get less and less angry as time passes.

Resentment
Resentment is a kind of slow-burning anger that can build up over a long period. Young people often feel resentful if one of their parents dies: there may new responsibilities which you don't want to – or feel unable to – take on. You may resent the extra help at home that you are expected to do, and resent your parent for asking you to do it. You may resent your friends their easier life with two parents. Remember, though, that you need your family and friends around you, so try not to let resentment come between you and spoil your relationships.

Guilt
People very often feel guilty after the death of someone important to them. You may catch yourself thinking 'If only ...': if only you had been kinder to them in the last few months; if only you hadn't parted on a bad note; if only you had been able to tell them that you really loved them. This regret is a natural part of the grieving process. It is a way of reviewing the past and trying to make sense of it. You may feel more guilt and self-blame if you have argued a lot with the person before their death. Try not to feel guilty about this, though, because such arguments are a normal part of your growth into an independent adult.

Worries and fears
The death of someone close to you can also make you fearful about the future. The world may seem a very unsafe place to be in: who will be the next person to fall ill, or have an accident, or die? Maybe even you? These worries and fears are again quite normal, and they do get less strong over time.

Time is such an important factor with so many of the feelings described above. You need time to express the feelings, time to work them through, and a lot of time before they stop dominating your life.

✣ In groups
Discuss what you learn from this article about the different feelings people who are bereaved have and why they have them.

30

Funerals

Different cultures and religions have different mourning customs. Whatever form the funeral service takes, it is important because it is the public recognition of the end of the person's life. Everyone who has loved or known the person gathers together to show how they cared for him or her and to share their grief. Some people express their grief by crying, others don't. A funeral is a sad occasion, but it is also an occasion to remember and celebrate the person's life.

> ❝ When my gran died, the funeral was really moving. It was sad, of course, but her best friend gave a speech about what a fun person she'd always been and they played her favourite music. ❞
> – Gianne

In pairs

Sometimes young people are not expected to go to the funeral or are prevented from doing so by adults. What are the arguments for and against letting young children attend funerals? Who should make the final decision – the children themselves or their parents? Does it depend whose funeral it is or how old the child is?

In groups

Study the article 'Showing emotions'.

Why is it important to cry if you feel like crying?

Why is it a good idea to talk to someone about your feelings?

Showing emotions

How should you express your feelings of grief when someone close to you has died? Should you let it all out – but for how long? Should you keep it under wraps and hope it will go away?

We all have different ways of showing our feelings. Not everyone wants to cry a lot; some people are very quiet and hide their feelings; other people like to talk about the person who has died. Often we are told what feelings to have, or how to show them, but this can be very different from what we actually feel.

We may be told by our parents or relatives to be 'brave' or 'strong'. There is a long tradition in many western countries for people to suffer grief in private, not to burden others with it or to be too emotional in public. But this isn't necessarily the best way to deal with difficult feelings, nor is it the only way. The tradition in many other parts of the world is for people to cry in public, to be openly emotional and to share their feelings with others.

It is certainly not a sign of weakness if you feel like crying. Indeed, it can be a sign of deep feeling. It is also a great relief and it can help other people to show their sympathy for you. So you should definitely cry if that is what you feel like doing. The expression of grief through your tears may bring you a lot of relief. Nor is there a set time by which you are supposed to have 'got over' your grief. People vary enormously in how long they need to show their emotions and to grieve. All we can say is that as time goes on, the need to cry will not be as strong.

However, there are other ways of grieving than crying. You shouldn't think that just because you are not crying you are not grieving. Thinking about the person you have lost is a way of grieving. And so is thinking about how the world is now that they aren't there for you. Talking about these thoughts and feelings may be difficult, but it is good to try, as it will move the process on and give you some relief.

There are other ways of showing our emotions which are less helpful, such as being destructive or very negative towards others. It can be very tempting, especially for young people, to express your feelings in actions rather than words. But talking about your grief instead is a more appropriate way of dealing with the difficult feelings inside. It is also much more helpful to you.

You and your feelings – dealing with loss

Helping the bereaved

It can be hard to know how to help someone who is grieving. Here's a test to help you understand how you can support someone who has been bereaved.

Can you help a friend in need?

1 When your friend brings up the subject of the person who has died, the best thing for you to do is …
   a Listen.
   b Try to change the subject.

2 When you see your friend for the first time after they've been bereaved, the best thing you can do is …
   a Avoid the subject of bereavement at all costs.
   b Say something about the death as soon as you meet.

3 Your friend and her family would probably appreciate …
   a A quick call to ask if there's anything you can do to help.
   b A bit of peace and quiet with no interference from people outside the family.

4 When should your friend have got over the grief?
   a After six months.
   b Probably never.

5 If you do write a card or letter, it's more comforting to …
   a Include a little note sharing some memories.
   b Simply sign your name rather than write a message.

6 If you're one of the first people to find out what happened, you should …
   a Keep the news to yourself.
   b Let other people know as soon as possible.

Answers BELOW

Answers

1 (a) Listen. It's important to let them know you are there if they'd like to talk about their feelings, or about the person who has died, even if you didn't know them.

2 (b) Say something. Don't avoid bringing up the subject when you first meet for fear of 'reminding' your friend about their grief. Let them know you're aware of the situation and that you're ready to lend support.

3 (a) A quick call. Why not ask if their family would like you to help with practical things? It could be anything from offering to sort out shopping to keeping an eye on pets when they attend the funeral, but every little bit helps.

4 (b) Probably never, although things will improve as time goes by. Don't lose patience with your friend if you feel it's taking too long for him or her to get over the grief. Take more time to listen and talk things over.

5 (a) Write a note, saying how sorry you are to hear the sad news. If you knew the person who died, you might like to share some memories you have of them.

6 (b) Let other people know. If you are one of the first to know, it's a good idea to let their other close friends know, so that they can offer their sympathy and support.

Someone to talk to

If you are upset about the death of someone close to you, you could contact Cruse Bereavement Care, a national charity which offers support to anyone who has suffered a bereavement.

Contact Cruse Bereavement Line 0208 332 7227

'People who contact us usually want to talk about the person who's died and we'll listen. They can say whatever they like about them. They'll often want to talk about other feelings surrounding the death – maybe they'll feel angry or wish they'd told them something while they had the chance.

'Everyone grieves in their own way, but when you feel ready, it can help to talk to someone – they can either be someone close or a stranger. Some people find it easier to talk to a stranger. Call us any time and we'll help you along the way.' – Cruse

In groups

Discuss what you learn from the advice on this page about how to help someone who has been bereaved.

Adapted from It Happened to Me *by Lesley Johnston*

Coping with rejection

Erica Stewart offers advice on how to deal with rejection

When a relationship breaks up, it can be a very painful experience, especially if it happens suddenly when you weren't expecting it. The shock you feel can be similar to the way you would feel if a close friend died.

Coping with rejection isn't easy, and if the relationship was a really good one, it's natural to feel grief that it's over. So don't feel that it's wrong to get some of the grief out of your system by having a good cry.

One thing people often do if they're rejected is to start asking themselves what went wrong. It is worth remembering that relationships end for all kinds of reasons and that it's rarely just one person's fault. Being rejected hurts and dents your confidence, but beware of looking for faults in yourself that simply aren't there.

Also, don't waste time trying to repair a relationship that's over. If you go round pleading with your ex-boyfriend/girlfriend to take you back, you're only prolonging the agony. Doing so is more likely to turn them off than win them back.

And try not to sit around brooding and letting yourself think that you'll never make another relationship. As you go through your teens, you're likely to experience a number of relationships. When a relationship ends, it can be difficult to tell yourself there'll be others. But there will be!

Time is a great healer. It might feel like you will never get over being dumped, but you will. Keeping busy helps. Make sure you arrange to go out with your friends and have some fun times. You may not feel like it, but it's better than moping.

🌐 In groups

Discuss the advice that Erica Stewart gives on how to cope with feeling rejected. Which is the most useful piece of advice?

Draw up a list of Dos and Don'ts when dealing with rejection.

ANNOUNCING IT'S OVER

The golden rule when ending a relationship is to make sure that you leave the other person's confidence intact. So try to avoid being too personal. If you're ending the relationship because you feel the other person has been too possessive or jealous, then it's worth saying so, since that may help them in future relationships. But if you've decided to end it because you've come to the conclusion you've been going out with a wimp, there's no need to say so. It's bad enough being rejected, without having to listen to a string of hurtful remarks.

Louisa Fairbanks

🔵 In pairs

Discuss what Louisa Fairbanks says about how to end a relationship. What's the best way to announce that you are ending a relationship – over the phone, through a friend, by writing a letter or face-to-face?

for your file

A penfriend has written to tell you that the person they've been going out with for over a year has ended the relationship and they are desperately upset. Write a reply offering them advice on how to cope with their feelings.

7 You and your body –

How dangerous is drugtaking?

Drug use can never be 100 per cent safe. It always involves risks, but it is not always as dangerous as some people make out. How dangerous it is depends on the drug itself, the person taking the drug and how and where the drug is taken.

The risk will also depend on:

How much is taken.

How strong the dose is, for example two ecstasy tablets which look the same may have very different doses in them.

How often it is taken.

What else might be mixed in with the drug, especially the rubbish that is often mixed with illegal drugs.

Whether drugs are being mixed together.

How a drug is taken; injecting is just about the most dangerous way to use drugs – the dose is taken all at once so there is a danger of overdose – if injecting equipment is shared, there is the danger of passing on infections like hepatitis and HIV (the virus that leads to AIDS). Eating a drug (as people sometimes do with cannabis) may also be risky because you might take a lot in one go and then it is too late to do anything about it.

THE PERSON

If you drink when you feel miserable, you will often feel worse; if you are anxious and depressed before taking LSD, you are more likely to have a bad experience. Also the following factors may influence the experience:

Physical health problems. Drug use could be more dangerous for those with heart, blood pressure, epilepsy, diabetes or liver problems.

Weight. Drugs act differently depending how heavy you are: the effects may be more in a lighter person. People who have eating disorders like anorexia or bulimia may also find drug use makes it even worse.

Not being used to drugs. Somebody new to drug use may be anxious, unsure of what to do or expect and be more likely to get into problems or have a nasty experience.

Sex. Drug use may be different for males and females because of the different way people view male and female drug use. It is often seen as OK for men to do certain things or behave in certain ways but not for women.

THE DRUG

Different drugs carry different risks.

Drugs such as heroin, alcohol or tranquilisers can lead to **physical dependence or withdrawal symptoms.**

Drugs like amphetamine, ecstasy and cocaine are **uppers** – they speed the body up – and can be particularly dangerous for people who have heart or blood pressure problems.

Drugs like heroin, alcohol and solvents are **downers** – they slow the body down – and can be very dangerous if mixed because the body can stop altogether. This is an overdose and can be fatal.

Others are **hallucinogens** (LSD, magic mushrooms) and can lead to people freaking out and doing dangerous things. Anybody with a mental illness should steer well clear of these drugs and cannabis as well.

THE ENVIRONMENT

Where people use can be risky. Some take drugs in dodgy places, like canal banks, near railway lines, in derelict buildings. Accidents are much more likely in these places especially if people are out of their heads. Also if anything does go wrong it is less likely help will be at hand or an ambulance could easily be called.

What people are doing while they are on drugs can be risky. Driving a car or bike or operating machinery while on drugs can greatly increase the chances of accidents. Having sex while on drugs can make remembering safer sex – like using condoms – much more difficult.

SO WHAT DOES ALL THIS MEAN?

It means that it is impossible to make simple statements like 'If you take this drug then this will happen.'

We are all individuals – what might be safe for one person could be dangerous for the next – or even dangerous for the same person in a different situation.

From *D-Mag*

In groups

Discuss what you learn from this page about the different factors which affect how dangerous drugtaking is.

for your file

Write an article for a teenage magazine based on the information on this page explaining what makes drugtaking a risky business.

drugs and drugtaking

Solvent abuse

Solvents are the least glamorous of drugs but are among the most lethal. Solvent abuse kills more people than heroin and ecstasy put together but we hear less about it.

What are solvents?

They are chemicals found in everyday household products such as aerosol cans (things like air freshener, hairspray, insect killer and deodorant), lighter fuel, glue, correction fluids like Tippex, paint thinners or strippers and petrol.

What is solvent abuse?

Some people use solvents as a drug – to change the way they feel and behave. Solvents are misused in a number of ways. Aerosols and lighter fuel can be sprayed directly into the mouth which is particularly dangerous. Most glues are used by inhaling the fumes and vapours from a plastic bag. Paint thinner is more likely to be sniffed from a cloth.

Why do people abuse solvents?

Most young people abuse solvents to get 'out of it'. Reasons include boredom, curiosity and peer pressure. Some young people abuse solvents to try to forget about other serious problems such as bullying or family troubles. Solvents are cheap and easy to get hold of. Young people who would be refused alcohol and cigarettes in shops because they are under age find it easier to buy solvents.

Solvents can seem less of a threat than other drugs – especially as the deaths they cause are not so widely reported.

What happens when solvents are taken?

The feeling is a bit like being drunk, but does not last for very long – sometimes only a few minutes – unless more solvents are taken straight away. Users can feel light-headed, dizzy and more adventurous. Sometimes they can black out for a while or feel drowsy, sick or out of control. Some people see or hear imaginary things (this is called hallucinating).

What are the side effects?

Headaches, sickness, skin irritation and rashes. But sometimes the effects can be more serious.

Can you die from abusing solvents?

Yes. People can die from fainting and choking on their own sick. Others die from heart failure or from being unable to breathe after squirting aerosols or gases straight down their throats. Or they die in accidents, especially when using solvents in risky places far away from help, such as by canals, in disused old buildings, on roof tops, or by train lines.

Is solvent abuse against the law?

No. Neither is under-age smoking or drinking. But shops and pubs are not allowed to sell alcohol to anyone under 16. It's much easier to buy solvents. People of any age can buy them. Shopkeepers can be prosecuted for selling solvents to people under 18 if they think they will misuse them, but it's often hard for shopkeepers to tell.

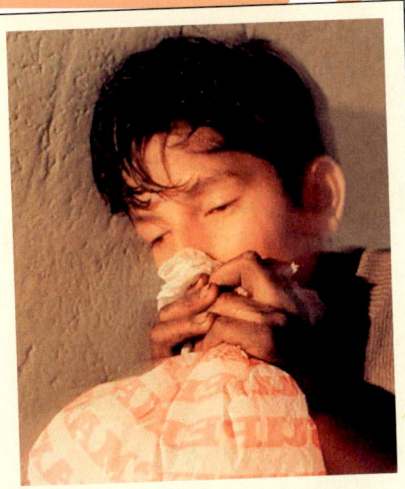

Are there any ways to reduce the dangers of solvent abuse?

No. There is no such thing as 'safe sniffing'. Other drugs are at least made specially for humans to take, but lighter fuels, glues and aerosols are not. They are designed to glue things together, or freshen the air in your room.

Adapted from *Sniffing Disaster* by Emily Moore

In pairs

Study the article 'Solvent abuse' then produce a list of key facts about solvent abuse – 'Ten Things You Should Know About Solvent Abuse'.

You and your body – drugs and drugtaking

Drug problems

'My Life's a Mess'

Name: Sarah **Age:** 16 **Lives:** Suffolk

I used to think I'd never take drugs. I was happy enough – what did I need drugs for? If only things had stayed that way...

The first time I took speed I just wanted to try it once – to see what it was like. We were going to this party, and my friends said that we'd have a better night if we were off our heads. I can't remember much about the party now. I felt so tired afterwards – really done in.

Drug buddies

I started going out with these friends quite a bit – they knew where all the good parties were. We'd meet up on a Saturday night and take some whizz to see us through. We were having a brilliant time. My other friends at school seemed really immature and boring.

Out of control

After school, we'd meet up and smoke some spliffs. I could never be bothered to do any homework when I got home – I always felt so tired. When I failed the end of year exams I had this massive row with my Dad. I hated being at school and I hated being at home. I started stealing money from my mum's purse to pay for the drugs and the nights out. I knew I was letting her down – but it had got so I only felt good when I was off my head on something.

Disaster

There was this big night out planned. I wanted to try some E – but I was broke. me and a mate went into town and nicked some stuff from one of the department stores. I was really scared. We thought we'd got away with it, but then the store detective came up to me – it was the worst moment of my whole life.

Shunned

The police told my parents – and now my Dad won't speak to me. He says he never thought his daughter would turn out to be a thief. My friends at school have found out about the shoplifting and some of them are keeping away from me. I don't know how all this happened. I never thought I'd be in trouble with the police. It's going to take a long time before people trust me again – I just wish everything was back to normal.

From Drugs – The Facts, Health Education Authority

How to help a friend who has a problem with drugs

We all need friends. Sometimes we need the help they can give us. Sometimes it's our turn to help them out. If someone you know has a problem with drugs ...

- Stick by them. Don't turn your back on them.
- Listen to them and how they say they feel.
- Don't start slagging them off to their face or other people.
- Suggest what they might do but don't keep on about it. They will have to make their own decisions.
- If they want, offer to go with them if they are going to seek help from a drug agency, doctor, counsellor or whoever.
- Encourage them to be positive about themselves.
- Encourage them to feel they can do something positive about their problems.

From D-Mag

In groups

Discuss Sarah's story. Talk about how getting into drugs has affected her life. If you were Sarah's friend, what would you say to her to try to help?

for your file

'Dear Melanie, My friend's got involved in the drug scene. She's got real problems. How can I help her?' Shania

Write the reply you would send to Shania if you were Melanie.

What to do in an emergency

Drug use can be dangerous and it's important that you know what to do in an emergency. The lives of friends and people around you could depend on you knowing basic first aid.

If people are tense and panicky

This tends to occur with hallucinogenic drugs like LSD and magic mushrooms, but it also happens with drugs like amphetamines and ecstasy as well as high doses of cannabis. If someone is really tense and panicky on drugs take the following steps:

✔ Calm them down and reassure them.

✔ Talk quietly and explain that the panicky feeling will gradually go.

✔ Keep them away from loud noises and bright lights.

✔ Help them if they overbreathe (hyperventilate). When someone breathes very quickly and gasps for breath, they often get dizzy and feel sick.

If people overheat or dehydrate

This tends to happen with drugs like amphetamines and ecstasy when people really exert themselves. These drugs raise body temperature. If people use these drugs in hot places, like clubs, body temperature goes even higher.

These drugs give an energy boost and people often dance for long periods, getting even hotter. As they get hotter they lose a lot of body fluids – as much as a pint an hour.

Overheating and dehydration can result. This can be very dangerous and has been the main reason for ecstasy-related deaths.

The warning signs include: ● cramps in the legs, arms and back ● failure to sweat ● headaches and dizziness, vomiting ● suddenly feeling very tired ● feeling like a wee but not doing much when you go ● fainting.

It can be prevented by:

✔ Avoiding amphetamines or ecstasy in the first place.

✔ Not dancing for long periods at a time; taking regular rests and relaxing in a cool area.

✔ Drinking water, fruit juice or a sports drink at about the rate of one pint an hour (sipping the drink regularly) and avoiding alcohol.

✔ Drinking or eating something that keeps the salt levels in the body up. Salty snacks, fruit juice, fizzy drinks and sports drinks will all help to keep the body provided with the minerals it needs.

✔ Wearing cool clothes and not wearing hats (hats keep heat in).

If someone is overheating:

✔ Move the person to a cool area – outside if possible.

✔ Splash them with cold water to cool them down.

✔ Call an ambulance. Explain to the ambulance crew what has happened and what you have done.

If people are drowsy but conscious

This usually happens with downer drugs like alcohol, tranquillisers and heroin, but can happen with solvents (glue and gas). If someone is really drowsy take the following steps:

✔ Put the person in the recovery position and keep talking to them.

✔ Try to stop them becoming unconscious and don't put them to bed as they might lose consciousness in their sleep. (People have been put to bed in a drowsy state only to be found dead the next morning.)

✔ If they want a drink only give them sips of lukewarm water. DO NOT give anybody black coffee. This just makes the drugs in them work even faster.

✔ Call for medical assistance.

If people faint or lose consciousness

Give them emergency first aid, by putting them in the recovery position, checking their breathing and loosening any tight clothing that might restrict it, and call for an ambulance.

for your file

Write an account of an incident involving a teenager who becomes ill after taking drugs. Describe how the person is given emergency first aid by their friends.

From D-Mag

8 You and the law –

Young people and crime

Why do so many young people commit crimes?

One in three crimes of burglary, theft and criminal damage are committed by people under the age of 17. Most of these crimes are committed by boys.

There are many reasons why some young people commit crimes. Here are some possible answers.

1 On television, and in adverts and magazines, young people are encouraged to spend, spend, spend. They are told there is a certain way to look, a certain way to impress others. There is a lot of pressure on young people to behave in a certain way – these pressures force some young people into crime.

2 Many people have very little money. Yet they live in a society which says money is important. If you've got no money and no prospects of a job or future, then crime might seem an attractive alternative.

3 Some people have very unhappy childhoods – violence at home, broken marriages, difficult parents. These can lead to some young people expressing their anger and frustration through crime.

4 For others, life seems boring and meaningless. They commit crime because it brings adventure and risk into their lives and makes them feel they've got a purpose. They reach a stage where they don't care if they get caught – anything is better than a boring existence.

5 For some young people a life of crime makes them feel important. They feel different from other people – it makes them feel big. If a person belongs to a group or gang, they may feel that being involved in crime will gain them respect in the group.

From Introducing Moral Issues by Joe Jenkins

More girls turn to crime

Girls in Britain today are 11 times more likely to be convicted of crime than they were 50 years ago, according to a report which shows that juvenile crime overall is nearly three times higher than half a century ago.

Jan Walsh, head of the Consumer Analysis Group which compiled the report, said: 'The rise in female juvenile crime is perhaps the most fascinating aspect in the report.'

She added: 'I believe the commercial society is a root cause. There is a much greater emphasis on what we possess today. From the earliest age, through television advertising and peer pressure, children are persuaded that they must possess all kinds of things. It is now a very basic fact of a young person's life. They must have the right trainers on their feet and the right logo on their backs. This didn't exist fifty years ago. In those days children made do with hand-down clothes.'

Others argue that there is a difference in the way children are brought up. Girls fifty years ago had much less freedom. Consequently they were much less likely to get into trouble.

Adapted from How Children Have Changed in 50 Years by Celia Hall

⊕ In groups

1 Discuss the reasons why young people commit crimes. Which of the five reasons given in the article above do you think is the main reason? Can you suggest any other reasons?

2 What does Jan Walsh mean by 'the commercial society' (see article, left)? Do you agree that young people are put under pressure to have possessions from an early age?

crimes and punishments

Shoplifting

A survey of youth crime reported in March 2000 that shoplifting came second to fare dodging as the most commonly committed crime.

Why do people do it?

There are many reasons why people shoplift. Greed is one, but some people do it because they find it exciting. Others are forced into it to finance a drug habit, but shoplifting can also be an act of desperation by someone who needs clothes or food and has to steal out of necessity.

One of the most common reasons among teenagers is peer pressure. Perhaps your friends have encouraged you to do it for a laugh or because they do it and you think you should too. But remember, shoplifting, even if it's as small as a packet of chewing gum, is a criminal offence. And just because some of your mates manage to get away with it doesn't mean you will too. If you are spotted you'll have to live with the shame of being caught and having a criminal record. So when you're tempted, ask yourself, 'Is it really worth it?'

Rebecca's story
"Getting caught was so humiliating"

I first started shoplifting properly when I was 12, although I'd stolen things like sweets before that. I started nicking because most of my mates used to do it in their lunch hour. We'd hang around the local shopping precinct and for a laugh see what we could steal. We'd roll up magazines and walk straight out of shops with them or stick make-up up our shirt sleeves.

Half the time we nicked things we didn't even want – things like those little clothes dyes – because it was a laugh just to see what we could get. But when one of my mates nearly got caught we stopped for a while. In fact, after that most of us were too chicken to carry on. I thought I was really good at it though, and because I got a real kick out of getting away with it I kept going.

I was so confident about robbing stuff that it never really crossed my mind that I might get caught. But one day last November I got a real shock.

One afternoon I bunked off school and went to steal some make-up. I used my usual technique to distract the assistant's attention and thought I'd got away with it. But as soon as I went through the exit a security guard grabbed me by the arm. He was really rough with me and I was practically dragged through the store with loads of people staring at me. I felt completely humiliated.

I was taken to an upstairs room to see the store manager. I thought he'd be okay if I made up some story and started crying, but he just didn't want to listen to me. I tried to tell him it was all a mistake but he told me I'd been filmed walking out of the store with goods I hadn't paid for and that another shopper had also witnessed me putting make-up up my shirt sleeve.

I was asked to turn out all my pockets and to undo my sleeves. I had three lipsticks on me that I hadn't paid for, and I had no receipts or anything. When I tried to talk to the manager he just said, 'You can talk to the police when they get here.'

From *Mizz*, issue 253, © Mizz/IPC Syndication

✤ In groups

1 Discuss why Rebecca started to shoplift. What do you think are the main reasons why young people shoplift?

2 What is your attitude to shoplifting? Is stealing from a shop any different from stealing from an individual or from someone's home?

3 'Modern shops make shoplifting too easy.' What do you think shops and shopkeepers could do to cut down shoplifting?

4 What should shopkeepers do if they catch a shoplifter? Should they always call the police whatever the circumstances? Give reasons for your views.

for your file

Write a story about a young person who is caught shoplifting.

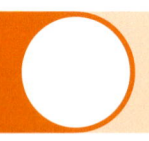

You and the law – crimes and punishments

Punishment

The aims of punishment

A person who is found guilty of a criminal offence will be given a punishment by the court. There are five main theories of punishment, each of which has a different purpose (see table).

⊕ In groups

Discuss the five theories of punishment. What do you think the most important aim of a punishment should be?

Theory of punishment	Aim of punishment	Examples of punishment
1 Deterrence	To stop the offender from doing it again; to discourage others from committing a similar offence	A prison sentence or a heavy fine
2 Protection	To protect society by making it impossible for the offender to commit further offences	Long prison sentences for dangerous offenders; banning dangerous drivers
3 Reform	To help the offender change their behaviour, so that they will stop committing crimes	Many sentences for young offenders, e.g. community service orders
4 Retribution	To make the offender suffer for the crime	Sentence proportionate to severity of the crime, e.g. at least five years for rape
5 Reparation	To repay or compensate the victim	Compensation orders and reparation orders

Imprisonment – does it work?

Taking away a person's liberty by giving them a custodial sentence is sometimes regarded as the best way not only to deal with people who have committed a serious offence or who are habitual offenders, but to teach a young offender a lesson. However, there is evidence from research studies to suggest that harsh punishments do not necessarily work. Instead of deterring a person from committing further crimes, a period of imprisonment may make them feel resentment towards society, so that on their release they commit further crimes in order to get their revenge. Whatever the reason, a large number of those who are given custodial sentences re-offend following their release.

⊕ In groups

❝ Prisons are necessary because they keep criminals out of circulation. ❞

❝ You've got to have prisons because no other form of punishment acts as a sufficient deterrent. ❞

❝ Community service is a better punishment than prison, because offenders are doing something to help the community. ❞

❝ A prison sentence is more likely to turn a younger offender into a criminal than to reform him. ❞

Discuss these views and say why you agree or disagree with them. What do you think should be the main reasons for giving someone a prison sentence?

A country without prisons

Imprisonment has never been used in Greenland, the world's largest island.

'We don't believe in punishment,' said Miles Pederson, a lay magistrate at the high court in Nuuk. 'We achieve more by trying to re-socialise people. Locking someone up for 10 years isn't going to make them a better person.'

Only those considered 'a danger to society' are sent to the Herstedvester closed prison in Denmark.

Fewer than 1% of criminals in Greenland reoffend. 'Closed prisons are simply factories for new criminals. This system makes it possible for people to change their lives and return to society,' said Yoan Meyer, the chief constable of Greenland.

Adapted from *The Guardian*, 13 September 1999

Types of punishment

The punishment that can be given for any particular crime is determined by the law. So the punishment for the same crime can vary from country to country. For example, in Britain drug dealing is punishable by imprisonment and/or a fine, while in some countries it is punishable by death.

⊕ In groups

Study the cases below. Imagine that each person has been prosecuted and found guilty in court. What punishment would you regard as appropriate in each case – **a)** if it is the person's first such offence, **b)** if the person already has a record suggesting that they are often in trouble?

1 A 20-year-old convicted of selling ecstasy and cocaine.
2 A 16-year-old who was found drunk and disorderly in a public place.
3 A 15-year-old who took away a car and crashed it causing £5000 worth of damage.
4 An 18-year-old who mugged a middle-aged woman and stole her handbag.
5 A 15-year-old who was caught shoplifting a pair of designer trainers.
6 A 25-year-old convicted of rape.
7 A 17-year-old convicted of being in possession of a knife.

What about the victim?

Some people argue that the punishment should fit the crime and take into account the effect the crime has on the victim. In some cases, the effect of a crime on a victim may be out of all proportion to the crime itself. For example, the theft of £10 may completely destroy the confidence and security of a woman living on her own. On the other hand, the theft of £20,000 worth of goods from a large wholesale company may make only a very small dent in the accounts.

⊕ In groups

1 How do you decide which is the more serious crime? Should the burglar who stole £10 be punished more severely because of the effect on the victim? Or should the thieves who stole £20,000 get a heavier punishment because the value of the property stolen was so much greater?
2 Some of the victims of crime are relatively helpless (for example, a disabled older person, a young child). Should the severity of the punishment take into account who the victim was, or should there be a standard punishment for a particular type of crime, irrespective of who the victim was?

A dictionary of punishments
Here are some forms of punishment used in modern societies.

Attendance centres – part of the offender's leisure time must be spent here.
Binding over to keep the peace – the offender's parents must look after their child properly or face a fine.
Capital punishment – the death penalty.
Community service order – unpaid work for the community.
Compensation order – payment made by the offender to the victim.
Conditional discharge – no action is taken on condition that the offender does not reoffend within a set period.
Confiscation of property – goods or possessions are taken away.
Corporal punishment – beating or other physical punishment.
Custodial sentence – prison or other secure accommodation.
Disqualification – from driving, for example, or from holding office.
Fine – the amount depends on the offence, the age of the offender, their history and their ability to pay.
Probation order – the offender must be supervised by a probation officer and usually attend a day centre.
Reparation order – the offender must compensate the victim or the community in some way.
Supervision order – the offender must be supervised by a social worker or probation officer.

You and the law – crimes and punishments

How can crime be reduced?

The high level of crime is one of the major problems facing society. This page examines some of the ways that have been suggested of treating young offenders to cut down the amount of youth crime.

Tough sentences

Opinions are divided on the effectiveness of giving young offenders a custodial sentence in a detention centre with a strict regime. Some people think that giving young offenders a short, sharp shock will deter them from committing further offences. Others argue that such treatment does not have the desired effect and that there is no evidence that it actually reduces the number who re-offend.

Surveys of young offenders, however, suggest that giving them harsher treatment at detention centres does have a deterrent effect.

Conservative MP John Greenway is in favour of tougher sentences: 'We have to crack down hard on young offenders. We cannot afford to be soft. We must teach them crime is not acceptable.'

Twenty-four-hour monitoring

In the USA schemes to monitor persistent offenders round the clock have cut crime. Similar schemes have been introduced in some parts of England. Mentors check on the offenders at any time of day or night and, if they cannot account for their movements, they are taken back to court.

One area where the scheme has been introduced is Rotherham. 'The aim is to keep them out of trouble and get them to take court orders seriously,' says Pat Booth, head of Rotherham's youth offending team.

'The youngsters have to tell us what they will be doing seven days a week. We will check on them at any time of day or night. If they are supposed to be at school or work we will check on them there.'

Naming and shaming young offenders

Youth courts now have the power to name persistent teenage offenders, who would previously have had their identities protected. They have been given such powers in the hope that naming and shaming young people will deter them from re-offending.

However, the courts have so far used these powers in a very limited way. Many people are concerned that publishing the names of young offenders may seriously damage efforts to rehabilitate or reform them, by giving them a bad name. Others feel that having their names made public only gives persistent young offenders the wrong sort of notoriety.

Making young criminals face their victims

Making young criminals meet their victims face to face, apologise to them and make some form of reparation has helped to cut crime in some regions.

The young offender, their parents and victims who are willing to take part are brought together in a meeting at which the consequences of the crime are discussed and the offender is made to apologise. If appropriate, the young offender may be made to pay back the victim in some way, for example, by repairing the damage they caused.

⊕ In groups

Discuss these ways of dealing with young offenders. Which do you think is the most likely to be effective in reducing crime? Do you have any other suggestions on how to treat young offenders in order to reduce crime?

Estate projects cut crime

CRIME and fear of crime have dropped in districts ranging from Swansea to Bradford, after the formation of Youth Action Groups. On a vandalised Bradford estate, emergency calls dropped from more than ten a week to nil after a youth team spent six months working with a gang that had targeted a parade of shops.

'We understand where they [gang members] are coming from,' says Julie Rhodes, 19, a recruit on the Bradford project. 'We know what they get up to,' adds Gavin Sunderland, 18, getting ready to go out on patrol. 'We probably like the same music they do too, which helps.'

From *The Guardian*, 30 May 2000

Cutting Under-Age Sales

King Alfred's Youth Action Group, formed at a school in Dorset, developed a project aimed at reducing under-age sales of tobacco, alcohol and solvents to young people in the Shaftesbury area. Members of the group, supported by Dorset Police, approached local agencies, including Trading Standards and Environmental Health, to seek their involvement in the project.

The Action Group, together with their partners, set up the innovative Responsible Retailers Scheme. This involves local retailers and publicans agreeing to follow guidelines drawn up by the partner agencies to reduce sales to under-age young people.

The scheme has resulted in a marked decrease in requests for under-age sales of tobacco and alcohol. It has also resulted in a decrease in the verbal abuse received by retailers when under-age sales were refused.

From the Home Office Crime Prevention website, July 2000

Don't Ignore Crime – Take Action!

'If we want to live our lives free from crime, we must recognise that we all have a responsibility to help reduce it.' Jack Straw, Home Secretary

What does taking responsibility mean? Does it extend to 'having a go' – intervening to prevent a crime if we see one being committed? Here two different viewpoints:

> *We live in a 'walk on by' society. If people see something going on, for example, an act of vandalism, they don't want to take the risk of getting involved because they're afraid of being either abused or attacked. But the only way to stem the rising tide of crime is for everyone to take a tougher stance. We must change our attitudes and our behaviour and be prepared to get involved, otherwise levels of crime will continue to increase.*

> *It's all very well to encourage people to have a go and to praise people who do so. But it's risky to intervene even in a low-level crime situation.*

Youth Action Groups

The aim of Youth Action Groups is to involve young people in projects that will reduce crime.

In groups

Discuss what you learn from the two articles about how Youth Action Groups have helped to reduce crime. Talk about other projects that Youth Action Groups could develop – for example, projects that might reduce the amount of vandalism or graffiti in your area.

As a class

Use the internet to visit the Home Office Crime Prevention website (www.homeoffice.gov.uk/crimeprev) to find out about other Youth Action Group projects. Contact your local police to find out about any youth projects already existing in your area. Then together discuss your ideas for forming a Youth Action Group at your school and get your class representative to put your proposal to the school council.

In groups

If you see a crime being committed, should you 'have a go'? What are the risks involved? Discuss the circumstances in which you think you should intervene.

9 You and other people –

Assertive, aggressive or passive

Everyone has to learn how to deal with difficult situations. Whatever situation you are faced with, there are three ways you can react. You can be either **assertive**, **aggressive** or **passive**.

Let's say that you've made an arrangement to meet a friend and they turn up half an hour late. There are three ways you could behave:

- You could get angry and shout at them. That's being **aggressive**.
- You could say nothing and bottle up your feelings, even though you're furious. That's being **passive**.
- Or you could calmly but tactfully tell them that you're feeling very fed up with them, because they've kept you waiting. That's being **assertive**.

Learning to be assertive will increase your self-esteem, because you can stand up for yourself and express how you feel. This will make you feel more confident in being able to deal with difficult situations.

If you are constantly being aggressive, people will think of you as rude and arrogant and are less likely to hear what you are trying to say. If your behaviour is passive, they may start to take advantage of you, thinking that you'll just do what they want.

In pairs

1 Study the article 'It doesn't pay to be passive'. What other reasons are there why people sometimes behave passively rather than assertively? What does Erica Stewart say are the consequences of behaving passively?

2 Discuss any situations in the past in which you have behaved passively and how you feel about having done so.

It doesn't pay to be passive

Erica Stewart explains why people don't always assert themselves and what the consequences are.

When we're faced with a difficult situation, it can be easier to say nothing and do nothing, rather than to speak up and say what we really feel. But taking the easy way out can leave us feeling angry, disappointed and frustrated, so why do we do it?

There are two main reasons why we don't stand up for ourselves. First, there's a fear of failure, particularly if we're dealing with someone who is older than us or in a position of power or authority. What if we try to put our point of view, or to make a request, only for it to be brushed aside or dismissed?

The other reason we may choose not to say what we think or feel is because we're afraid there'll be a scene. We're anxious about how people will react, and worried that they'll get angry and take their anger out on us.

The trouble is, if you don't do or say anything, nothing will change. You're left feeling upset and the situation may even get worse. If you don't tell people what's bothering you and why, you're not giving them the chance to do something about it. How can they know what you think if you don't say?

So it's far better to grit your teeth and say what you feel. At least you'll feel you tried, even if you don't seem to get anywhere. And that will also help to build your self-esteem.

being assertive

Assertive, aggressive and passive behaviour

Assertive behaviour
You are prepared to ask for what you want.
You express your feelings directly and openly.
You behave calmly and politely.
You stand up for your rights.
You behave confidently.
You acknowledge and respect other people's feelings.
You listen to and consider what other people say.
You are willing to negotiate and compromise.
When you want something, you explain why.

Aggressive behaviour
You demand what you want.
You express your feelings loudly and rudely.
You behave angrily and threateningly.
You tell people what your rights are.
You behave selfishly and arrogantly.
You don't respect other people's feelings.
You don't acknowledge that other people may have their own viewpoints.
You are stubborn and unwilling to compromise.
You tell people what you want, but you don't explain why

Passive behaviour
You don't ask for what you want.
You do not express your feelings openly.
You behave submissively.
You don't stick up for your rights.
You lack confidence.
You are too mindful of other people's feelings and try to do nothing that will upset them.
You take too much notice of what other people think and say.
You agree with anything in order to avoid confrontations.
You rely on others to know what you want.

In pairs

Study the table (above) and discuss the differences between assertive, aggressive and passive behaviour. Then study the situations listed on the right. For each situation write down what would be:
a) assertive behaviour,
b) aggressive behaviour, and
c) passive behaviour.
Then join up with another pair and compare your answers.

Role play

In pairs choose one of the situations and role play it in three different ways to show the difference between an assertive, an aggressive and a passive response.

1 You lend a friend a CD. She keeps on saying she's going to give it back, but she's now had it for a fortnight.

2 A group of friends have bought some alcohol. They offer you a drink, but you don't want one. They start to pressurise you to have one.

3 A friend is really pleased with their new sweatshirt, but you think it's old-fashioned and doesn't really suit them.

4 A teacher wants you to audition for a part in the school play. You are having trouble keeping up with your schoolwork and don't really want to audition for the part.

5 Your parents want you to spend the weekend with their friends who have a teenager your age. But your interests are totally different and you know from past experiences that the two of you won't get on.

6 You're a vegetarian and you are at a barbecue. You notice that the person doing the barbecue is using the same utensils for the beefburgers and the veggie burgers.

7 You are with a group of people and some of them start making racist remarks.

8 You are out with someone who suddenly starts taking things in a shop. They put one of the items in your bag.

9 You feel your boyfriend/girlfriend is becoming jealous and possessive, but you don't want to break off the relationship completely.

10 Your friend is very unhappy because they are going through a bad patch. They are biting their nails until they bleed and other people are making remarks about it.

45

You and other people – being assertive

How to be assertive

How to be Assertive

Being assertive is about having the confidence and skills that enable you:

- **To express positive feelings**, for example, to give and receive compliments, to ask for help and make requests, to approach people and begin conversations, to show affection and to express appreciation.

- **To express negative feelings**, for example, to tell people you are feeling hurt and why, to show and explain justifiable annoyance.

- **To stand up for your rights**, for example, to refuse to be pressurised into doing something you don't want to do, to make complaints, to express personal opinions, to reject unfair criticism and put-downs.

To be assertive you need to know what you want to say and how to say it. You also need to choose the right moment to say it. If you don't choose the right moment, you may fail to get your message across. For example, if your mum is getting ready to go to a business meeting and is running late, it's hardly the best time to ask her for a pocket money rise.

Say No and Mean It

If you really don't want to do something, don't allow yourself to be pushed into doing it. Use your body language to help you to refuse. Stand up straight with your head up to show that you aren't afraid. If appropriate give an explanation, but don't get drawn into an argument. Don't apologise for refusing and don't allow any taunts to get to you. Just say 'no' and keep repeating it until whoever it is accepts your decision or you move away from them. Remember that real friends will respect you more for being your own person and not bowing to pressure than they will if you give in and do something you didn't want to do.

Repeating the Message

This is a technique that you can use if you feel someone isn't listening to you or is deliberately trying to lead the conversation in a different direction in order to refuse your request or ignore your point of view. You keep on repeating the same sentence or phrase over and over again so as to get your message across. It is particularly useful:

- when you want someone to recognise your right to feel the way you do;

- when you want to refuse to do something; or

- when you are being denied your legal rights, for example, by a shopkeeper who is refusing to exchange faulty goods or to give you a refund.

Assertiveness Dos and Don'ts

DO Be honest. Say exactly what you are feeling and why.
DON'T Throw out vague hints, hoping the other person will know what you mean.
DO Stick to the point and keep returning to it.
DON'T Allow yourself to get sidetracked.
DO Treat the other person as an equal and listen to their point of view.
DON'T Try to bully, threaten or try to get your own way by making the other person feel guilty.
DO Speak clearly and use body language that suggests you are confident.
DON'T Mumble, shuffle awkwardly or avoid eye-contact.
DO Use an appropriate tone of voice.
DON'T Plead, whine or shout.
DO Choose an appropriate moment.
DON'T Start demanding to be listened to when it's clearly the wrong time.

for your file

Study the list of assertiveness Dos and Don'ts. Think of a difficult situation that you have had to deal with and write about how you handled it. Were you assertive? Did you handle it as well as you could have done? If you were to be in a similar situation again, what would you do differently?

Saying What You Want – Confidence Tips

The snag is, once you've decided what you really want, you still have to get the message over to someone else. This is never easy. As a young person you very often feel lacking in power, but there are tricks to feeling more confident and to help you grasp some of the power and control for yourself.

Step 1: Understand that everyone feels like this
This is a hard idea to swallow, but it happens to be true. Practically everyone feels shy, embarrassed, self-conscious or out of control at some time. The people you most admire for being self-possessed and assured are probably just very good actors. And acting is what confidence is all about. It's a trick, an image that people manage to put across that works so well it gives the user the confidence they crave.

Step 2: Decide what you want to say
Obviously when you tackle somebody about a difficult or sensitive problem there's going to be a lot of talk and probably a lot of emotion, but you should have in your mind one simple clear phrase or idea you want to get over.

Step 3: Get your message across
You also have to make sure that your message is delivered in a very direct way. You may not be feeling very good about yourself but you are sure about the idea you want to get across. Standing in a corner mumbling it at your shoes won't help anyone. Looking the other person in the face and saying it directly to them makes you look and sound self-assured and confident. If you can't look into the other person's eyes, then focus on a point between their eyebrows. Holding their gaze for just a few seconds will add a tremendous amount of power to your words.

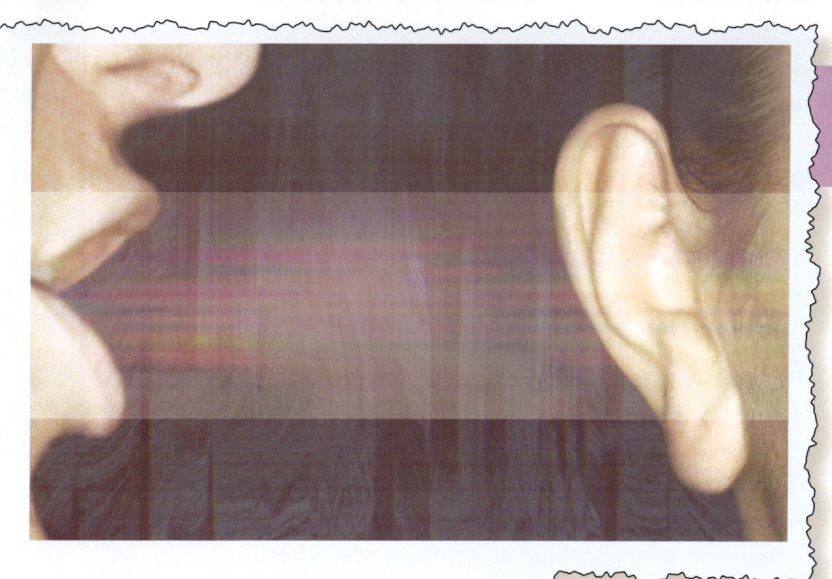

Step 4: Keep it short, keep it simple
It's very tempting when you're feeling unsure of yourself to dress up your message in lots of meaningless words like: 'Well, I was just wondering, if you really don't mind, it's just that I thought perhaps it might be a good idea ...' These are all very nice things to say, but they aren't going to help. They also prolong the agony. So look the person in the eye and say what you have to say clearly and simply.

Step 5: Acknowledge their feelings – but keep going back to the message
What you have to say is going to have some emotional effect on the other person. They may be surprised, shocked, angry or whatever, and start shouting at you or trying to argue with you. Stand firm. Acknowledge their feelings, for example, 'I know that you're upset about this, but ...' and then go back and repeat your message.

Step 6: Don't get angry
Try to keep the emotional temperature as normal as possible. If the other person starts getting angry or extremely upset, try saying, 'Please don't be angry, this is something we need to discuss.' Say it calmly and keep on saying it. If you really can't get anywhere, then tell them you'll just have to discuss it later when they are feeling more calm.

Role play

In pairs develop a series of role plays in which you take it in turns to practise being assertive. Here are some possible situations:

1. You take some faulty goods back to a shop and ask the manager for a refund.
2. You ask your parents if you can go to stay with a friend who your parents don't particularly like.
3. A friend is pressurising you to do something you don't want to do.

In groups

1. Study the advice in the article (left). Which piece of advice is the most helpful?
2. Who is it easiest to be assertive with – your parents, your brothers and sisters, your friends, strangers?

Adapted from *Say What You Mean and Get What You Want* by Tricia Kreitman

10 You and the media –

The press in Britain

The power of the government

Many of our views and ideas are influenced by what we read in newspapers and magazines. Because the press has such power to influence public opinion, in some countries it is controlled by the government. People can only read the news and get the information that the government wants them to have.

In Britain, as in other democracies, there is a free press. Newspapers and magazines are run by privately owned companies. They are financed by advertising and sales and compete with each other for readers.

However, even in a democracy such as Britain's, the government does exercise some controls over the press. During national emergencies it may censor reports. Also the government will sometimes issue a D-notice, or defence notice, to newspaper editors requesting them not to publish reports on certain subjects in the interests of national security.

The power of the owners

It's not just the government that controls what you read in the press: newspaper owners do so too.

Ownership of Britain's most popular national newspapers is concentrated in the hands of four companies which together account for 85% of the sales of daily newspapers. The largest company, Rupert Murdoch's News International Corporation, which owns *The Times*, *The Sunday Times*, the *Sun* and the *News of the World*, accounts for 41% of all daily and 45% of all Sunday newspaper sales.

Newspaper owners, or proprietors, have tremendous power to influence the political message that their papers give. Traditionally, popular papers such as the *Daily Mail* and the *Daily Express* have supported the Conservative Party, while the *Daily Mirror* has supported the Labour Party.

The power of the Sun

Until it was bought by Rupert Murdoch in the 1970s, the *Sun* supported the Labour Party. It then became a fervent supporter of the Conservative Party. The paper claimed to have played an influential part in the Conservative Party victory at the 1992 election by running a series of anti-Labour stories. After he became Labour leader in 1994, Tony Blair set about winning the *Sun*'s support: he went on to win the 1997 election.

In groups

1 Is it right for newspaper proprietors to have so much control over the political message that their newspapers give?

2 Should there be limits on how many papers a company is allowed to own, for example, only two national newspapers?

News management

A lot of news comes from big businesses and government. They want newspapers to portray them in a positive light, so they use public relations specialists to help them in their dealings with the press.

Political parties have become increasingly skilful at what is known as 'spin doctoring': presenting their news in a way that makes their policies appear successful and gives them good publicity. They are also skilful at distracting attention from things they do not wish to get too much media coverage. For example, they often time their press releases so that a positive story hits the headlines on the same day as a negative report is to be issued.

the power of the press

What controls the content of newspapers?

While the views of owners have a considerable influence on the content of newspapers, they are by no means the only factor. Another very important influence is consumer demand. Newspapers have to provide readers with what they want to read, otherwise they wouldn't sell enough copies. So a newspaper like the *Sun* contains lots of human interest stories and few international news stories, because that's what the readership wants.

Another commercial factor is the need to attract advertisers. The revenue from advertising is crucial to newspapers. So the stories they contain must attract the audience that their advertisers want. They must also be careful not to include stories that might offend the advertisers.

The editor and journalists of a newspaper also have to decide on how newsworthy a particular story is. The amount of space given to a report will depend on what the journalists consider to be the news value of the issue or topic.

⊕ In groups

Study two or three different newspapers for the same day. What are the main stories in each paper? Compare the different amounts of space they give to particular stories. What do you learn about the news values of the different newspapers?

⊕ In groups

"Celebrities shouldn't moan about the press. If you're a public figure, then you've just got to accept the fact that people are interested in you."

"People have a right to their privacy. There should be a privacy law to protect people from press harassment."

Discuss these views.

Public interest versus Private rights

Politicians, pop stars, princesses — the roles carried out by all these people means that they attract a great deal of media attention. Most of them thrive on it, but when journalists begin to ask questions about their private lives, they are usually less keen to be in the spotlight. When does media interest become an unacceptable invasion of privacy?

For some journalists, especially those working for the tabloid newspapers, the issue is a simple one:

'The acid test of whether a story should be published is simple: Is it true? If it is, and the truth hurts, that is no argument for suppression.' The Sun newspaper

Diana, Princess of Wales, spent all her adult life in the glare of the media. Editors knew that they could increase circulation simply by putting a photograph of her on their front pages. When she was killed in a car crash in Paris in 1997, while trying to evade photographers, there was a strong public feeling that the media had killed her. There were calls for stronger laws to protect people's privacy but the key problem of balancing the right to privacy with the 'right to know' remains.

The issue becomes even more complicated when public figures try to have the best of both worlds, being paid by gossip magazines for photographs of their family wedding, for example, but complaining about media attention on other occasions. Is it reasonable to expect the media to take an interest in people's private lives only when it suits those involved?

Adapted from Media Power by Alison Cooper

You and the media – the power of the press

Young people and the press

Kids: What the papers say

A research study of 400 articles from one week's newspapers has found that children are often presented as stereotypes by the press. A team of children, members of Children's Express, a charity where children spend their free time learning journalistic skills and reporting on children's issues, found that children appear over and over again in very specific categories.

The most common stereotype, found in one third of all the stories, was the 'kid as victim', usually sanctified no matter how they have previously behaved. The researchers argue that this gives a very false picture. 'It highlights the whole adult stereotype of children being weak,' said Sharon O'Dea, 17.

Over a quarter of the stories presented the stereotype of the 'cute kid', who has little news value, but provides the feel-good factor and often an engaging photograph. 'Kids in these photographs are just being used,' said Curtis Anderson, 15. 'The kids aren't getting anything out of it.'

More than 10 per cent of the stories the team examined demonised children – tales of evil children, young hooligans, bad parents put on the line by their kids. Mehrak Goldstein, 14, was particularly angered by this. 'The press hears a story about bad children, they give out the bare facts and they don't give it a second thought. The kids aren't given a chance to explain themselves.'

Less prevalent but still very evident are the 'kids are brilliant' stories in which children excel in some way, getting into Oxbridge at 10 or donating their pocket money to the Third World. These stories were judged as very patronising.

There are also the 'kids as accessories' stories, where children are used to somehow enhance their parents; and the 'kids these days' category, which includes stories about children being corrupted by computers and teenage pregnancies, with adults commenting that it never used to happen in their day.

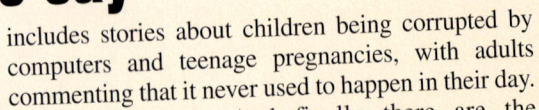

And finally there are the 'brave little angels', children who endure terrible illnesses with a smile, or risk their lives by hauling a toddler back from a cliff edge.

But how serious is this stereotyping, and does it affect the lives of ordinary children? Gerrison Lansdown, director of the Children's Rights Development Unit, says: 'The role the media plays in constructing stereotypes is hugely influential in the way we see the world. For example, on Channel 4's Look Who's Talking programme featuring children, one lad of about 16, of very big build, said that even though he is a pacifist, people look at him, assume he's a thug and cross the road because he fits an image of thugs as presented in the press.'

Adapted from *The Guardian*, 8 April 1998

In groups

1 Discuss the seven stereotypes that the researchers identified. Have you come across any articles or stories recently that presented any of these stereotypes? How serious a problem do you think stereotyping of young people in the press is?

2 Go through some recent newspapers and study the articles they contain about young people. What images of young people do the articles give? Report your findings in a class discussion.

Teenage magazines

What do you think of teenage magazines?

Teenage magazines are designed and written by adults. Are you reading what you actually want to read or are you reading what adults think you want to read?

What teenagers say:

'Teenage magazines are patronising. They seem to think that all teenagers are interested in are pop stars, fashion, soaps and sex.'

'All the magazines are for girls. Why aren't there any magazines for boys?'

'Teenage magazines are entertaining and fun. I don't think they really have much influence on what we think.'

'There should be more articles written by teenagers for teenagers about serious matters.'

'Teenage magazines exploit teenagers. They do the fashion and pop industries' advertising for them, encouraging us to want things we don't need and can't afford.'

'You can learn a lot about life from teenage magazines — from things like the problem pages and readers' true experiences.'

What the editors and magazine journalists say:

'We're providing teenagers with what they want. If we didn't we'd go out of business because they wouldn't buy the magazines.'

'There's plenty of opportunity for teenagers to have their say. We're always interviewing them and running articles based on readers' responses.'

'Of course some of the articles are trivial, but so is a lot of life and it's our job to entertain, not educate.'

'We don't create teenage culture. That's done by TV and films and the pop business and the fashion industry. We have far less influence than they do.'

'We're sometimes criticised for having too many articles about sex. But we provide teenagers with a lot of information that they wouldn't otherwise get.'

'It's wrong to say there aren't any magazines for boys. There are lots of special interest magazines. Those are the ones boys buy.'

In groups

1 Discuss the comments about teenage magazines. Talk about their content. Do they provide what teenagers want? Are teenage magazines patronising? Do they manipulate teenagers' tastes and fashions? How much influence do you think teenage magazines have?

2 Draft a proposal for a new teenage magazine. Draw up full details of its contents and then present your ideas to the rest of the class.
Compare your ideas for new magazines with the magazines that are currently produced for teenagers. In what ways are your magazines different? How does your view – the teenager's own view – of what teenagers want to read differ from the adult's view?

for your file

Make a detailed study of a teenage magazine. Analyse its content, working out how much space is devoted to particular features, for example, fiction, pop, sport, hobbies, letters, social issues etc. Draw a pie-chart showing how the content of your magazine is divided. Write a few sentences saying what you have learned from your study about what the magazine editors think teenagers are interested in.

11 You and your money –

Bank accounts

Banks – What do they offer?

What's the best way to manage your money? More and more young people are deciding to put their money in a bank account. So what do banks offer young people and how do you choose which bank account to open?

Security Your money is safer in a bank than it would be in a drawer in your bedroom. And you don't have to carry large amounts round with you all the time, so there's less risk of it getting stolen.

Access There's easy access to your money if it's in a bank account. If you've got a passbook account, you can go into any branch of your bank and draw money out or pay money in at any time the bank is open. If you've got a cash card account, you can draw money out either from a bank branch or a cash machine.

Interest Accounts for young people are usually savings accounts, so you'll be paid interest on your money while it's in the bank. The rate of interest you get varies from bank to bank, so it's worth shopping around before opening your account, to find out which bank offers the best rate of interest.

So you want to open a bank account? Your questions answered

Q *How do I open an account?*

A You'll need to complete an application form, then take it to the bank, together with some form of identification, such as your birth certificate or passport. You'll also need to confirm your address, which you can do by taking a gas, electricity or telephone bill addressed to your parent or guardian. And you'll need some money to pay into the account. There's often a minimum deposit, usually either £1 or £10.

Q *How can I keep track of what's in my account?*

A If it's a passbook account, you'll have an up-to-date record of when you've drawn money out and how much is left in your account. If it's a cash card account, you'll be sent a full statement on a regular basis, often every three months. You'll probably also be able to get mini-statements on request or from a cash card machine.

Q *How often is interest paid?*

A Interest is usually paid quarterly or twice a year. But remember that interest rates change, so it's worth checking them now and again so that you can work out how much interest you're going to get.

Q *What happens if I lose my cash card? Can someone else use it?*

A With a cash card you are given a PIN (Personal Identification Number). That's to protect you against fraud, if you lose your card. So don't tell anyone else your PIN number or even write it down anywhere – just memorise it.

If you lose your card, report it to the bank at once. Then they'll stop the card, and no one will be able to draw money from your account, until you've got a new card.

In pairs

Discuss what you learn from this page about bank accounts and say whether or not you think it's a good idea to have a bank account.

for your file

A friend is thinking of opening a bank account. Write to them explaining the advantages of having a bank account and what you have to do to open one.

banking and ways of saving

Which Bank Is Best For You?

Armed with £40 to deposit, 15-year-old Claire Perrin checked out what the banks had on offer in January 2000.

Royal Bank of Scotland
Account name: Rate 15 account (for 11–15-year-olds)
Minimum deposit: £1
Cash card: £50 a day limit with Cirrus (for getting money out abroad)
Interest: 4%
Statement: Every three months
Other benefits: 20% off at HMV. Welcome pack with personal organiser
Claire's comment: 'The HMV offer was tempting, but I'm not sure I'd ever use Cirrus.'

Lloyds TSB
Account name: Under 19s savings account
Minimum deposit: £1
Cash card: £200 a day limit
Statement: Every three months. Instant mini-statement from cash machine
Interest: 3%
Other benefits: Free gifts vary from branch to branch
Claire's comment: 'There were, in fact, no free gifts.'

Barclays
Account name: BarclayPlus account (for 11–16-year-olds)
Minimum deposit: £1
Cash card: £50 a day limit
Interest: Tiered interest – 1.5% on £10–£99; 2% on £100–£249
Statement: On request
Other benefits: Paying-in book so you can use counter service. Online magazine with star interviews and competitions
Claire's comment: 'An on-line magazine is not much use if you haven't got a computer.'

Halifax
Account name: Expresscash account (for 11–15-year-olds)
Minimum deposit: £10
Cash card: £300 a day limit
Interest: 4%
Statement: Instant mini-statements from cash machine
Claire's comment: 'No welcome pack and I didn't feel there was much going for teenagers.'

HSBC
Account name: Live Cash account (for 11–15-year-olds)
Minimum deposit: £1
Cash card: £100 a day limit
Interest: 3.75%
Statement: Monthly. Mini-statement and balance on request
Other benefits: Free CD voucher. Welcome pack including personal organiser, diary, pen and dictionary of banking terms
Claire's comment: 'The free CD voucher and welcome pack enticed me.'

Abbey National
Account name: Action Saver (for 10–15-year-olds)
Minimum deposit: £1
Cash card: £500 a day limit for over 13s by application
Interest: 4% (higher rate for serious savers)
Statement: Twice a year
Other benefits: Twice-a-year magazine called The Mag
Claire's comment: 'The only reason to sign up here would be if I had any money to save.'

NatWest
Account name: CardPlus account (for 11–20-year-olds)
Minimum deposit: £1
Cash card: £250 a day limit with SOLO (which checks your balance before allowing you to buy things)
Interest: 4%
Statement: Monthly
Other benefits: £10 JJB/Sports division voucher
Claire's comment: 'Offering SOLO was a big plus – it would be great for shopping.'

In groups

On your own decide which of these bank accounts you would choose and why. Then explain your choice in a group discussion.

Adapted from 'Banking on it', T2, The Daily Telegraph, 22 January 2000

You and your money – banking and ways of saving

Other ways of saving

If you're a serious saver, then there are many other ways of saving your money besides opening a bank savings account. These two pages describe a number of these ways of saving. Some of them offer higher interest rates than bank savings accounts, but often you will only benefit from them if you leave your money in them for a considerable length of time – several months or several years. While some of them may be appropriate for you now, others are designed for adults and may not be suitable for you until you are older.

A national savings ordinary account

This is a savings account with two rates of interest – the standard rate for accounts with a balance of less than £500 and a higher rate for accounts which have over £500 invested in them. It is run by the Post Office and appeals to many people because you can use your passbook at any one of more than 18,000 post offices.

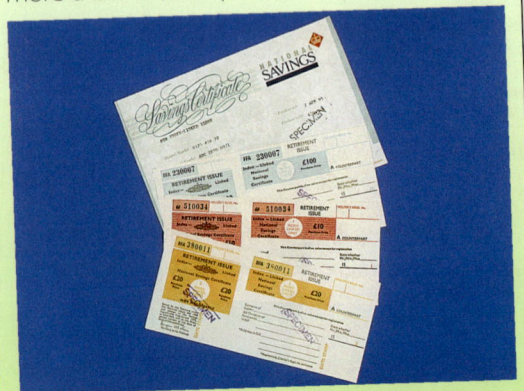

National savings certificates

You can buy national savings certificates at any post office. The certificates increase in value at a guaranteed rate over a number of years. Some people prefer this form of saving because the rate of interest is either fixed or guaranteed to beat inflation.

Premium bonds

Premium bonds offer you the opportunity of winning tax-free prizes. There is a jackpot prize of £1 million every month. The precise number of prizes each month varies according to the size of the prize fund. The prize fund for June 2000 was approximately £48.9 million and there were over 650,000 prizes. The odds of any £1 unit winning a prize are 20,000 to 1.

You can buy premium bonds at any post office. The minimum for each purchase is £100. Purchases over £100 are in multiples of £10. Anyone can own premium bonds but you have to be 16 before you can buy them for yourself. If you're under 16 they can only be bought for you by your parents, grandparents or guardians.

If you put your money into premium bonds, you can take it out whenever you want. But the drawback about premium bonds compared to other ways of saving is that your money doesn't earn any interest.

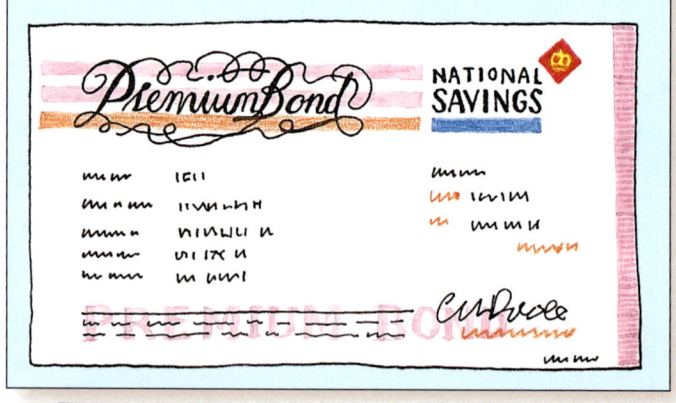

Building society accounts

A building society savings account is very like a bank savings account. But there are lots of different types of account and you can earn higher interest rates by putting your money into an account and leaving it there for several months or years. For example, you can get an account which allows you only two withdrawals a year. Other accounts will pay you a bonus if you don't make any withdrawals during a year.

Building societies offer people loans called mortgages to help them buy their own homes. They are more likely to offer a loan to someone who has shown that they can handle their money responsibly, so adults who are saving up money for a deposit on a house often put it into a building society account.

ISAs – Individual Savings Accounts

ISAs are offered by many financial institutions, such as banks and building societies. They offer a form of tax-free savings for adults who would otherwise pay tax on the interest they earn from their investments. There are restrictions on the amount of money each individual can save in ISAs each year. In 1999–2000 the maximum amount you could put into ISAs each year was £7,000.

ISAs: Invest as little as £1 and watch your tax-free return grow

Stocks and shares

You can invest in the stock market by buying shares. When you buy shares in a company you own part of that company. The price you will have to pay for each share will depend on which company you are investing in. You can find the price of a company's shares in the finance section of a daily newspaper.

If a company does well, you will get paid a share of the profits each year. This payment is known as a dividend. The size of your dividend will depend on how many shares you own. Also, if the company is doing well, the value of your shares may go up. If so, you would be able to sell them for more than you bought them for.

However, if the company does badly, then the value of your shares will go down. If you sold them you would get less than you paid for them. If the company was to go bankrupt, you could lose all the money which you paid for the shares.

Life insurance

Many adults take out life insurance policies. In addition to providing protection for their families in the event of their death, a life insurance policy can also be a long-term way of saving for the future.

A whole-life insurance policy can be taken out quite cheaply. The person whose life is being insured pays the insurance company a certain amount each year. If they die, the insurance company agrees to pay a sum of money to whoever benefits from their will. You can insure your life for thousands of pounds with a whole-life policy, but it is not a way of saving. The money only gets paid if you die.

Other forms of life insurance can be used as a way of saving. You make regular payments, called premiums, to the insurance company each month. In return, the company agrees to pay a fixed sum of money either when you die or when you reach a certain age.

In groups

Discuss the advantages and disadvantages of the different ways of saving that are described on these pages. Choose two ways of saving that you would recommend – one for young people, one for adults.

In pairs

A relative offers to buy you £100 worth of national savings certificates or £100 worth of premium bonds, on condition that you do not take the money out until you are 18. Say which form of savings you would choose and why.

for your file

Work with a partner. Go through the articles in this unit and pick out all the financial terms that are used in them, such as balance, dividend, premium, inflation. Write out definitions of them, if necessary using a dictionary to help you. Then put your glossary of financial terms in your file.

12 You and your body – eating disorders

Eating disorders – anorexia

Anorexia Nervosa

What is anorexia?

Anorexia nervosa is an eating disorder, often described as the 'slimmer's disease'. While the name means nervous loss of appetite, this is misleading. Sufferers of anorexia have not lost their appetite, but have lost the ability to let themselves eat food. They think about food, how they can resist eating and the way their body looks the whole time. Doctors define someone as anorexic when they have lost at least 15% of their normal weight, have a fear of fatness and think they look fatter than they really are. Anorexia is not a diet gone wrong. Anorexics are people with serious problems.

Who suffers from anorexia?

Over 700,000 people in Britain suffer from the disease. Anorexia most often occurs during adolescence in girls aged 12 to 17. But 1 in 10 sufferers is a boy. Boys are more likely to become obsessed by exercising than girls, and boy sufferers may spend every moment of the day exercising to burn off calories.

Is there a cure?

There is no pill which cures anorexia. Feeding a sufferer until they are of normal weight does not work. If this happens the sufferer will just go away and stop eating again because the original problems have not been solved.

In order to recover sufferers need to accept and like themselves, and they need to work on the problems that have caused their anorexia. It is difficult for sufferers to get better on their own. They need help from a doctor or from the Eating Disorders Association (see details, below). Some sufferers may need to go into hospital for a while, and they will need support from their family and friends. The sooner a person gets help, the quicker recovery will be.

Information and advice can be obtained from:
The Eating Disorders Association, Sackville Place, 44–48 Magdalen Street, Norwich NR3 1JU, tel: Helpline 01603 621414, Youth Helpline 01603 765050.

From Trouble with Eating by Emily Moore

PORTIA'S STORY

Portia's problems began around the age of 12 when she followed her sister to a weekly boarding school.

'I was homesick and unhappy from the start. I am naturally shy and self-conscious and did not keep up socially.' She was clever, though, and threw herself obsessively into academic achievement.

To the growing anxiety of her parents, she began to eat less and less. 'I rallied for a while, especially during holidays. Deep down, I think I knew what was happening, but could not relate it to myself. Working hard and not eating were distractions from feeling unhappy.' To her teachers, her academic success was welcome. However, there was little supervision of meals, so no one noticed her increasing absences.

Although Portia is convinced that thin role models in magazines and on television were not the root cause of her anorexia, she does believe that, once you are in the clutches of the illness or struggling to recover, they are not much help.

'My condition is like an addiction and television and magazines somehow reinforce it. To me, not eating is a way of controlling the real world, which is too intense to manage. So many people seem to think you are being selfish.' Almost tearful, she insists: 'It is not deliberate.'

From The Daily Telegraph, 20 June 2000

What causes an eating disorder?

There are no simple answers to what causes an eating disorder. In most cases it's a combination of different factors which cause a person to become ill. What is known is that some people are more vulnerable to eating disorders than others.

Perfectionism
Perfectionists – or rather, people who have unrealistic expectations of themselves and others – are more prone to becoming ill. This is because people like this feel inadequate and worthless no matter what they achieve. Everything in their lives becomes about 'being better' and often the pursuit of thinness is a part of this.

Control
Other people have eating disorders because they want to avoid something painful in their lives – perhaps a family problem or sexuality. Becoming locked in the behaviour patterns of a disorder helps them to bring an element of control to their lives.

Family Triggers
There has been a lot written and said about the role of families and eating disorders. What is known is that some people's families are overprotective and sometimes rigid in the way they deal with problems and conflict. When this occurs some people try to resolve their problems through what they do and don't eat.

Being Female
Girls are disproportionately affected by eating disorders because of the cultural demands on them for thinness. Men by contrast are still encouraged to be strong looking and may equate 'thin' with weak.

External Problems
Sometimes, external problems can trigger an eating disorder. For instance, bullying, sexual abuse, the break up of a relationship or moving home.

The Red Flags of an Eating Disorder

- 🚩 A desperate preoccupation with weight, shape, food, calories and dieting.
- 🚩 Overly and negatively fixating on looks.
- 🚩 Imagining problems would be solved by being thin.
- 🚩 An excessive and rigid exercise regime.
- 🚩 Avoiding situations when food is present.
- 🚩 Letting food and eating overshadow everything you do.
- 🚩 Desire to eat alone.

From Wise Guides – Eating by Anita Naik

Mark's story

Mark is 13 years old. He has been treated for anorexia but is still very thin.

'I didn't suddenly stop eating, it just crept up on me. I was always rather podgy in junior school and the other kids used to make fun of me because I couldn't run very fast. I was always one of the last to get picked for any team in games.

I had a stomach bug and lost a bit of weight while I was sick. I was rather pleased, so I decided to eat a bit less. I didn't bother much with dinner and my mum did evening classes and was always in such a rush, so she didn't really notice whether I ate tea.

I hoped that if I was thinner, I would be better at games and have more friends. But the other kids still made fun of me, because my legs got extremely thin.

My teacher phoned my mum about my weight and she took me to the doctor. I've seen loads of specialists and, when I got very thin, they put me in hospital. They tried to frighten me into eating by telling me I would die. In the end, I agreed to eat more so that I could come home. But as soon as I started putting on weight, I panicked and went back to not eating. I have dreadful rows with my dad about it, and he blames my mum. I just wish they'd leave me alone. It's my body.'

From Eating Disorders by Jenny Bryan

⊕ In groups

1. Discuss Portia's story and Mark's story. What triggered them to become anorexics? What do you learn from their stories about what it feels like to be anorexic and how anorexia has affected their lives?

2. Talk about the various different factors which may cause a person to develop an eating disorder. What do you think are the main reasons why people become anorexic?

3. Discuss how helping a person with anorexia involves not only getting them to eat enough food to stay healthy but sorting out the problem that caused them to become anorexic.

You and your body – eating disorders

Bulimia

What is bulimia?

Bulimia is an eating disorder which involves eating large amounts of food in a short period of time, then trying to get rid of it, for example, by vomiting it up.

Bulimics are often scared of the idea of gaining weight and will try to avoid food, then when the craving gets too much, they have a huge binge and try to get rid of the food afterwards by being sick, or taking laxatives which make them go to the toilet.

Bulimia can be a very difficult problem to spot. Bulimics often stay at a fairly normal weight and will eat quite sensibly and happily in front of friends and family. It's only in secret that they binge on all their 'forbidden treats' and then make themselves sick, and since they can be very, very clever at hiding what's going on, maybe not even their closest family will guess.

Even though bulimics don't usually starve themselves like anorexics do, they're still putting their health at risk. Over time, being sick so often will eat away at the sufferer's teeth and gums and could cause painful mouth ulcers and throat infections. Laxatives are tablets which speed food through the digestive system and out of the body. Many bulimics take these so that their body doesn't have time to absorb vitamins and minerals from the food it's given, and eventually body organs like the kidneys and heart can be damaged.

Just as important, though, is what damage bulimia does to the sufferer's happiness. They feel guilty and exhausted from hiding their secret and end up hating themselves more than ever.

What causes bulimia?

Bulimia begins because the person feels deeply unhappy inside. Usually they have a low opinion of themselves, feel a failure, or set themselves impossibly high standards that they feel they can't live up to. They hide their problems because they feel that admitting to them would be like admitting they're 'not good enough'.

Bulimics are nearly always female, and most often in their teens or early twenties. They're often people who are very bright and have close, loving families, but feel under pressure – maybe to do well at school, or to look a certain way, or from other problems.

When bulimics have a big food binge it isn't because they're greedy, and when they get rid of food by being sick or going to the loo, it isn't necessarily because they want to be thin.

Eating disorders are about using food to be in control. Teenagers face a lot of stress from exams, parents, friends, and just growing up in general, but often feel they have no power over their own lives. Sufferers may have been bullied or abused and made to feel powerless that way. They might decide without realising what they're doing that by making themselves sick they have some kind of control over their body.

What to do if a friend has bulimia ...

Don't accuse her
Just be there for her and make sure she knows she can tell you anything and you won't judge. Bulimics are very often people who desperately want to be perfect, so it can be hard for them to own up to having a problem. If she does confide in you don't feel you have to give her lots of advice – just listen.

Be patient
Hard though it is, you can't make her get help. That's got to be her decision. You can get books from the library or leaflets from the Eating Disorders Association to encourage her, but the rest is up to her.

Be positive
Bulimics already spend most of their time worrying about food, so try to show there's more to life. Don't discuss the problem as if that's the most important thing about her – get her out there and have fun, so she can feel like a normal person. You may find she's moody and irritable sometimes (through lack of a healthy balanced diet) so try to be understanding.

From *Shout*, issue 144, © D.C. Thomson & Co. Ltd

In groups

Discuss what you learn from this page about what bulimia is, what causes it and what you can do to help a friend who is suffering from it.

Eating disorders and the media

Skinny models 'send unhealthy message'

British doctors yesterday called on the media to use female models with more realistically proportioned bodies instead of 'abnormally thin' women who contributed to the rise in the numbers of people suffering from eating disorders.

A report by the British Medical Association claimed that the promotion of rake-thin models such as Kate Moss and Jodie Kidd was creating a distorted body image which young women tried to imitate.

'Female models are becoming thinner at a time when women are becoming heavier, and the gap between the ideal body shape and reality is wider than ever,' said the report. 'There is a need for a more realistic body shape to be shown on television and in fashion magazines.'

From *The Guardian*, 31 May 2000

Is there too much pressure to be thin?

Three young people express their views on how much pressure they feel the media puts on teenagers to be thin.

> I think there's an over-reaction to the effect that skinny models have on girls. We're not mindless idiots sucked in by every image fed to us. There are many other influences at work including peer-group pressure.
>
> When I see beautiful celebrities, of course, I think it would be lovely to look like them, but I'm over the fact that I don't match up to supermodels. I know now that magazines show impossibly perfect models in photos that have been touched up – a practice I feel should be banned.
>
> Anna Rose Sheppard, 19

> When it comes to pointing the finger, I don't think the media should shoulder all the responsibility. Friends and family are a bigger influence – and usually dieting is a sign of a problem more deep-rooted than just thinking you don't possess the perfect vital statistics.
>
> Lavon Hendricks, 16

> I try not to compare myself to slim models but it's hard because they're everywhere. Sometimes it does feel as if that's what you have to look like.
>
> I do wonder why some famous people have to be incredibly skinny to be successful. And it goes without saying that I prefer magazines that use real readers to model clothes; you just get a better idea of how things will look on you.
>
> Julie Kerr, 13

From *The Daily Telegraph*, 1 July 2000

In groups

1 Do you think there is too much media pressure on girls to be thin and to look like supermodels? Say why you agree or disagree with the views expressed by the three teenagers (right).

What about boys and their image? What media pressure is there on boys to look athletic and to conform to a certain body shape?

2 " *The secret of being a truly attractive person has nothing to do with your dimensions. Intelligence, personality, confidence and social skills (like how well you get on with people) all count far more when it comes to being a happy and therefore an attractive person.* " – Adele Lovell

Discuss Adele Lovell's view. How far is attractiveness what a person looks like? How much does it depend on a person's character and how they behave?

for your file

Write a statement saying how much pressure you think media images put on young people and which you think is more important – personality or looks.

13 You and the community –

How local government is organised

There are two different structures of local government that apply to different parts of Britain. In Scotland, Wales, Northern Ireland and parts of England there are **single-tier** authorities responsible for all local authority functions. In the rest of England, there is a **two-tier** system, in which responsibilities are divided between two separate councils – county councils and district councils.

Single-tier authorities

Unitary authorities:
- 22 Welsh unitary authorities
- 47 English shire authorities
- 32 Scottish unitary authorities
- 26 N. Irish unitary authorities

Metropolitan authorities: 36 metropolitan authorities (Metropolitan authorities serve areas around England's major cities.)

London boroughs: 33 London borough councils (London also has the Greater London Authority – see below.)

Two-tier authorities

County councils: 36 county councils
(County councils are responsible for education, social services, strategic planning and local transport. They also send representatives to the local police authorities and local health authorities.)

District councils: 238 district councils
(District councils are responsible for refuse collection, housing, local leisure facilities and planning within the local area.)

The Greater London Authority (GLA)
The GLA consists of the elected Mayor and the London Assembly, which has 25 members. Its main functions are transport, including control of the underground and London buses, strategic planning, economic development and, in conjunction with the London boroughs, improvement of the environment.

Town and parish councils
Most areas have town and parish councils. They have very limited powers, such as looking after town halls and museums and co-ordinating twinning visits with other towns.

How local government is financed

Local authorities raise their income in a number of different ways (see pie chart).

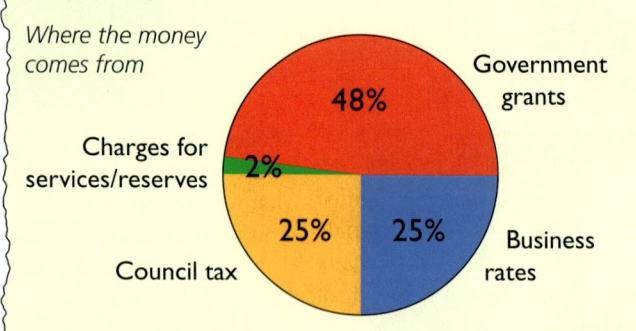

Where the money comes from

- Government grants 48%
- Business rates 25%
- Council tax 25%
- Charges for services/reserves 2%

Business rates are taxes paid by local businesses. The amount is proportional to the size of the premises that the businesses occupy.

Council tax is paid by individuals. The amount a person pays depends on how much the house is worth and how many people live in it. The idea is that the size of a person's house is related to their income.

Critics of the council tax system argue that it does not take into account people's ability to pay. They say that there should be a local income tax to finance local government. This would be directly linked to the amount a person earns.

Burning poll tax demands, 1990

🞉 In groups

1. Discuss how local government is organised and financed.
2. What is the system of local government in your area?
3. Which do you think would be a fairer way of paying for local government services, the existing council tax or a local income tax? Give reasons for your view.

local government and local organisations

Local authority services

Local authorities in England and Wales spend £65 billion a year providing services for 52 million people. These are the major services they provide:

- **Education:** Local authorities spend over £21 billion a year providing education for more than 8 million children in nearly 25,000 schools.

- **Social Services:** Social services departments spend £9 billion a year providing care and support for vulnerable people. They administer children's homes, arrange care for the elderly in their own homes and in residential care. They are responsible for adoption and fostering services for children, sensory impairment and disability services and many other services.

- **Planning:** Local authorities are responsible for planning the location of new development such as housing, industry, shopping and leisure facilities and of the transport systems to serve them.

- **Libraries:** There are 15,000 public libraries in England and Wales. Libraries are one of the most heavily used public services.

- **Waste Disposal and Collection:** Councils are responsible for the disposal of waste and the collection of waste from households.

- **Fire and Rescue:** Council-run fire services employ 20,000 fire officers in 1,286 fire stations in England and Wales.

- **Emergency Planning:** Emergency planning services ensure that the emergency services are ready to respond immediately to any disaster that might occur, such as flooding, a major accident, such as a chemical emission, or an aircraft crash or terrorist attack.

- **Roads and Highways:** Local authorities provide, manage and maintain more than 96% of roads in England Wales, as well as maintaining major parts of the motorway and trunk road network for the DETR, a service which costs almost £1 billion a year.

- **Housing:** Local authorities provide around 3.5 million homes in England and Wales at a cost of around £2 billion a year.

- **Environmental Health:** Environmental health services deal with matters such as food safety, housing standards, pollution control, animal health, Agenda 21 and noise control.

Difficult choices

All these services have to be paid for and each year they cost more to provide. Often councils are faced with difficult choices – either to raise the council tax, to cut some of their services or to increase charges for certain services. None of the solutions is popular but councillors are elected to make such decisions.

In groups

Imagine you are local councillors. You have to save money on this year's budget. The options are listed on the right – you may choose any three but the whole group must agree on your choices. Once you have decided, take it in turns for the groups to reveal their choices and the reasons for them to the rest of the class. Then hold a vote to decide which three actions your class would take.

1. Increase charges at the public swimming pool.
2. Collect refuse once a fortnight only.
3. Close down centres for older people to meet.
4. Close the public library at 5.00pm instead of 7.00pm every day.
5. Introduce charges for youth clubs.
6. Cut spending on the fire service.
7. Have fewer nursery classes for 4-year-olds.
8. Have fewer public health inspectors.
9. Increase charges for museum visitors.
10. Close down the local tourist office.

You and the community – local government and local organisations

Getting people involved in local government

At present, only a small proportion of those who are entitled to do so actually vote at local elections. The turnout at local elections is rarely above 40% and in some cases has been as low as 10%.

It has been suggested that one reason for this is because of the way local elections are organised.

In groups

1 'The whole system of local elections is far too complicated. No wonder people don't bother to vote.' Discuss this view.

2 Proposals for change include introducing yearly elections in most areas, making it easier to vote through new ideas like electronic voting, mobile polling stations, so that people can vote at places such as supermarkets, and voting on different days (such as at the weekend, rather than on a weekday).

Discuss these ideas for change. Do you think they will encourage more people to vote at local elections?

Local elections

The electoral arrangements for each type of authority are described below. All councillors serve for a term of four years.

Metropolitan districts are divided into wards, each of which is represented by three councillors. One-third of the seats are up for election each year for three years out of four.

District councils and English shire unitaries are divided into wards but they have a choice over their election cycle. They may either adopt the metropolitan district system, or all the seats on the council can be contested once every four years.

Welsh unitaries are elected every four years with a mixture of single and multi-member wards (about 50% are multi-member).

County councils are divided into electoral divisions with one county councillor representing each division. Elections are held once every four years when all the seats on the county council are up for election.

London boroughs are elected on a four-year cycle of the whole council. Most wards are multi-member.

Greater London Authority: London has a directly elected mayor who is elected using the SV (Supplementary Vote) system on a single London-wide voting area and serves for four years. The Assembly is elected using AMS (Additional Member System) and comprises 25 members who serve for a term of four years.

In groups

1 Discuss the idea of having directly elected mayors running councils. Do you think having mayoral elections will persuade more people to vote?

2 Are there any proposals for a directly elected mayor in your area? If you could vote in a referendum to have a directly elected mayor to run your local council, how would you vote? Explain why.

Bill paves way for directly elected mayors

Local communities will be able to elect a mayor to run their councils under plans unveiled yesterday.

A new Local Government Bill will require councils to introduce new ways of running their affairs, including a cabinet system for taking decisions rather than the traditional committee system of council management.

All local authorities, apart from parish councils, will be able to choose whether to move to a directly elected mayor with a cabinet; a cabinet with a leader; or a directly elected mayor with a council manager.

Where councils want to have a directly-elected mayor, they must put the idea to a local referendum.

Referendums will also be triggered if five per cent or more of the council's electorate present a petition for a mayor.

Ministers expect that major cities such as Liverpool, Birmingham and Manchester will be among the first to follow London in moving to an elected mayor.

They hope the prospect of having an American-style directly elected mayor will revive interest in local government and persuade more people to vote.

From *The Daily Telegraph*, 27 November 1999

Being a councillor

In groups

Discuss what councillors do. Would you ever volunteer to be a councillor? Give your reasons.

WHO CAN BE A COUNCILLOR?

Anyone can stand for election to the local council, provided they are over the age of 21 and have some sort of connection to the local area. This means that they either live in the area, own a business there or are employed there. However, some people are prevented from standing, such as employees of the local council, a person who is mentally ill or a person who has been declared bankrupt in the last five years. You don't have to be a member of one of the political parties; you can stand as an independent candidate.

What do councillors do? A county councillor explains

As well as attending council meetings, where we debate and vote on local issues, I sit on a number of committees. That's where a lot of the detailed decisions are discussed. I'm on the housing committee and the social services committee.

I also keep in touch with the people I represent by running regular surgeries. Anyone who has a problem with something that concerns the council can come to me for advice and I'll do whatever I can to help them.

I'm not paid for the work that I do and I'm not in favour of full-time paid councillors. I think it's important to have people from all walks of life on the council and I don't like the idea of having professional politicians running local government. But I'm not against change. I think directly elected mayors are a good idea. Lots of people don't know who the leader of the council is and if there was a cabinet they'd understand more who's in charge of what. Most people don't know who the chair of the committees are.

Being a councillor takes up a lot of time, but I don't regret it. I feel as if I'm doing something for the community.

Giving teenagers a voice

The teenager heading a new youth council has pledged to make young people's voices heard.

Fifteen-year-old Clair Linzey, from the Cherwell School, in Marston Ferry Road, Oxford, was voted in by the thirty-two 12- to 17-year-olds who sit on the committee.

The Oxford Youth Council was set up by the city council to keep them in touch with the views of young people in the city. Clair said that up until now youngsters had had no way of having their voices heard and she promised this would change.

'They have, in the past, assumed what we wanted. We needed a way of communicating. We can now be listened to and taken seriously,' she said.

'Young people do not all have the same views as their parents or each other, and issues such as homelessness and transport affect us too.'

From the Oxford Mail, 13 July 1999

In groups

Youth councils

Some local authorities have set up youth councils in order to involve young people in local matters (see article).

Is there a youth council in your area? Discuss the advantages of having a youth council. Talk about how it should be elected and what items you think ought to be on the agenda of its meetings.

for your file

Either write a letter to your youth council about an issue that you think it should put on the agenda at its next meeting, *or* write a letter to your local council explaining why you think it should set up a youth council.

63

14 You and your opinions –

Political parties and the political spectrum

A political party is a group of people who broadly share the same views about how a country should be governed. When we discuss the beliefs and policies of a political party we are discussing the party's political **ideology** – its ideas about the best kind of society to live in and how this can be achieved.

Political ideologies range from left-wing to right-wing. In general, left-wing parties are radical parties. This means they desire social and political change. Right-wing parties are usually conservative parties. They support traditional ideas and the retention of the existing social and political norms.

When we compare the ideologies of parties we place them on what we call a political spectrum. The political spectrum is a line which extends from extreme left to extreme right.

In groups

1. What is meant by the political spectrum?
2. What is the difference between left-wing parties and right-wing parties?
3. What are the main ideas and beliefs of communism, socialism, liberalism and conservatism?
4. What is fascism? Why do the vast majority of people find fascism repugnant?

Communism (left-wing) — centre — Fascism (right-wing)

Communism
The most extreme left-wing ideology is communism. It is regarded as a radical ideology because it aims to place all parts of the economy, that is, the production and distribution of goods and services, and all financial institutions like banks, under the ownership and control of the state. There is no private ownership under communist rule.

Socialism
In a socialist system, there is some private ownership of small businesses, but banks, transport and communication facilities, and the supply of power, health and education services are owned and operated by the government. It is claimed that this kind of social and economic system protects the workers from being exploited by unscrupulous employers.

Liberalism
Liberalism stresses the importance of the individual. Each individual has the right to lead his or her own life free from government restraints and control. Liberalism, therefore, argues that governments should not play a major role in the economy and should not interfere in society. Each individual should have the right, for example, to work as an employee without having to join a union, and to decide what he or she will watch or read without fear of government censorship.

Fascism
An extreme right-wing ideology is fascism. It demands the absolute loyalty and obedience of all citizens to the dictator and the political party which the dictator leads. Fascism champions capitalism, bans organisations like trade unions, identifies other races and peoples as inferior, and stresses the importance of the state or nation that will endure for centuries.

Conservatism
Conservatives believe in the strength of tradition. They are reluctant to change society. They therefore support the existing situation or the status quo.

Adapted from *You and Your Government* by Graham Shipstone

which political party do you support?

The three main political parties in Britain

This page gives details of the three main parties. Details of other parties can be found on page 66.

In groups

Study the list of key policies of the three main parties. Which of their policies do you most support? Why?

Labour Party
newLabour newBritain

Leader: Rt Hon. Tony Blair, Prime Minister

Formed: Beginning of 20th century

When in power: 1974–79 (in coalition with Liberals 1978), 1997–present

Number of MPs (2001 general election): 412

Key policies

Education: Invest more in classrooms and resources. Create specialist schools, which concentrate on one area, such as arts or sports. Expand higher education, funded through tuition fees.

Health service: Allow good performing hospitals to become foundation trusts, responsible for their own finances, and with greater freedom to make their own decisions. Bring down hospital waiting lists.

Taxation: No increase in income tax. Has raised national insurance and other indirect taxes to fund expenditure on public services.

Electoral reform: Considering further reform of the House of Lords.

Europe: Has postponed joining the single currency until the time is considered right.

Funding: By trade unions, individual membership and donations

Leading members of Labour: Gordon Brown, David Blunkett, Jack Straw

Conservative Party

Leader: Rt Hon. Michael Howard, Leader of the Opposition

Formed: End of 18th century (Central Office founded 1870)

When in power: 1970–74, 1979–1997

Number of MPs (2001 general election): 166

Key policies

Education: Greater role for private sector. Allow successful schools to expand by giving them more control over their admissions policies. Allow greater freedom for universities.

Health service: Tax breaks for those with private health insurance. Cut bureaucracy and waste.

Taxation: Reduce income tax in the long term. Opposes increases in national insurance.

Electoral reform: Firmly against. Supports first past the post system.

Europe: Against the single currency 'for the foreseeable future' and against the development of a federal Europe.

Funding: Largely funded by big business

Leading Conservatives: Lord Coe, Michael Ancram, David Davis

The Liberal Democrats

Leader: Rt Hon. Charles Kennedy MP

Formed: 1988

When in power: (as the Liberal Party) in coalition with Labour 1978

Number of MPs (2001 general election): 52

Key policies

Education: Invest in education by giving more power to local councils.

Health service: Abolish eye and dental charges. Opposes hospitals becoming foundation trusts and believes this money should be spent on front line care.

Taxation: Tax the super rich by raising income tax to 50p in the pound for those earning £100 000. In favour of abolishing council tax and introducing a local income tax.

Electoral reform: Supports full electoral reform by bringing in proportional representation.

Europe: Supports further development of the European Union.

Funding: By individual party members

Leading Liberal Democrats: Menzies Campbell, Simon Hughes, Matthew Taylor

You and your opinions – which political party do you support?

Other political parties

Scottish and Welsh nationalist parties

The Scottish Nationalist Party campaigns for independence for Scotland. Five Scottish Nationalist MPs were elected in 2001.

The Welsh Nationalist Party campaigns for an independent Wales. Since 1992 it has had four MPs in Parliament.

Northern Ireland

In Northern Ireland, the political parties are split into three separate camps. On the Unionist side are the parties which are firmly committed to Northern Ireland staying in the United Kingdom. These include the Ulster Unionist Party, with six MPs, and the Democratic Unionist Party with five MPs.

On the Republican side are parties that support a United Ireland. The Social Democratic and Labour Party (SDP) has three MPs. There also exists Sinn Fein, which has been described as the political wing of the IRA, which has four MPs.

There are two parties which are non-sectarian, which means that they do not support either the Unionist or Republican side. These are the Alliance Party and the Women's Coalition.

Fringe parties

There are also a number of smaller 'fringe' parties in the United Kingdom, none of which have any MPs, although they put up candidates at general elections:

- The Green Party, which campaigns for the protection of the environment.
- The National Front, a fascist party which argues Britain should be run by white British people only.
- The Socialist Labour Party which believes in a socialist economy.
- The UK Independence Party, which believes the United Kingdom should leave the European Union.
- The Monster Raving Loony Party, which protests against the entire political system.

In groups

Forming a political party

You have been given the task of forming a political party. This means that you will have to develop a number of policies which your group believes would be for the good of the country.

You will have to develop policies on the following issues:

? The economy
? The environment
? Transport
? Health and social welfare
? Europe
? Education

Give your party a name, which reflects its political ideology. Then take it in turns to present your party's policies to the rest of the class.

After you have presented your policies, discuss in your group how your party's policies were received by the rest of the class. Would you need to change them in any way so that in an election you would receive more support from class members?

Adapted from You and Your Government by Graham Shipstone

Taking a vote

In groups

Here are a number of statements on some contemporary social issues. On your own, decide whether you agree or disagree with each statement, and think about whether anyone you know or anything you've seen or read has influenced your opinion on that particular issue. Then share your opinions in a group or class discussion.

1. If a young person is unemployed it is because they have not tried hard enough to find themselves a job.
2. The possession of cannabis should be decriminalised.
3. There is too much sex and violence on television.
4. The women's movement has become too powerful and it is now men who suffer discrimination.
5. The monarchy should be abolished.
6. Capital punishment should be reintroduced for the crime of murder.
7. All forms of hunting should be made illegal.
8. Privatisation is a sound economic policy.
9. Everyone who earns more than the national average wage should have to take out a personal pension plan to provide them with an income in old age.
10. There should be stricter controls on asylum seekers and the granting of refugee status.

How would you vote?

On your own

Look again at what the different political parties stand for (pages 65–66). Decide which political party you would vote for if there was to be a general election tomorrow. Explain the reasons for your choice.

To vote or not to vote

Although everyone over the age of 18 can vote in a general election, approximately 27% of the electorate do not vote. A person who does not vote is said to abstain. People who abstain often come from one of the following five groups: poorer people, older people, women, younger voters and the least educated.

People abstain from voting for a variety of different reasons. Some of the reasons why they do not vote are:

- They may find themselves unable to agree with all the policies put forward by any of the parties.
- They may do so as a protest against the whole political system.
- They may not have faith in any politicians doing anything for them.
- They cannot be bothered.

People who do not vote often claim they do so because 'it won't make any difference'. But abstaining is important and it does make a difference, particularly if there is a closely fought contest and the winning candidate only wins by a few votes.

Role play

In pairs, act out a scene in which a young person tries to persuade another person, who has said that they do not intend to vote, that it is important for them to do so.

In groups

'It is everyone's duty to vote. Voting should be compulsory.'

'It is everyone's right to choose not to vote. To force people to vote when they choose not to do so would be to deny them their rights.'

Say which of these views you agree with and why.

15 You and your body –

Some young people have their first experience of sex without fully realising the risks that may be involved. As the newspaper report (right) shows, a lot of people who have sex at an early age regret having done so. The aim of this unit is to make you aware of what is meant by safer sex and to give you information about sexually transmitted infections (STIs).

What is safer sex?

There's no such thing as totally safe sex. There's always some risk involved. Safer sex means trying to cut down the risk of catching an infection. Although health experts can offer advice about sexual behaviour that is likely to keep you safe from disease, nothing is 100 per cent certain. That's why they talk of safer sex rather than safe sex.

14-year-olds 'regret having had sex'

A third of schoolgirls and more than a quarter of boys who have had sex have told researchers they regretted it.

Girls said being pressured into sex by their boyfriends was one reason for regret.

Boys said they wished they had not put pressure on their girlfriends.

Nearly a fifth of boys and 15% of girls, whose average age when they were interviewed was 14, said they had had sexual intercourse.

Research by the Medical Research Council and Public Health Sciences Unit in Glasgow supported the idea that early sexual intercourse was often regretted.

From *The Daily Telegraph*, 5 May 2000

'I never really thought about it. I knew my boyfriend had several other partners before me, because he was five years older than me. But when he wanted to have sex, I just let him because I knew otherwise I'd lose him. When I suggested he should use a condom, he just laughed and said he never bothered with things like that. It was only afterwards when I found out that he'd given me an infection that I realised how stupid I had been.'

Anna

Four rules for safer sex

Wait until you are ready. The first way of practising safer sex is not to have sex until you are absolutely sure that you are ready for it.

Never have unprotected sex. Whenever you have sex use a barrier method of contraception – the condom. Other methods of contraception can stop unwanted pregnancies but do not offer protection against sexually transmitted infections.

Stick to one partner. It's obvious that the fewer partners you have, the less chance you have of catching an infection.

Avoid high-risk sexual activities. The most risky activity is having unprotected anal intercourse. That's because during anal intercourse the anus easily becomes damaged, and any infected body fluids can then enter the bloodstream.

✠ In groups

1 What is meant by safer sex?
2 Why do adolescents run a greater risk of catching STIs?
3 Discuss Anna's experience. Do you think she was just unlucky in her choice of partner or do you think her boyfriend's behaviour was typical?

Adolescents are at risk

For the vast majority, sexual relations begin in adolescence. For a number of reasons, adolescents run a greater risk of getting a sexually transmitted infection.

✻ Experimentation is a normal part of adolescent development which also exposes them to health risks. Young people's sexual relations are often unplanned, sporadic and, sometimes, the result of pressure or force.

✻ Sexual relations typically occur before adolescents have gained experience and skills in self-protection, before they have acquired adequate information about STIs, and before they can get access to health service and supplies (such as condoms).

✻ Young girls are especially vulnerable for physiological, social and economic reasons.

Adapted from *Sexually Transmitted Diseases and Young People*, World Health Organisation

safer sex, STIs and AIDS

Sexually transmitted infections

SEXUALLY TRANSMITTED INFECTIONS

What are STIs?

Sexually transmitted infections or STIs are infections that are passed from one person to another during sexual contact. The infections affect the genital area, as well as the bladder, so they are known as genito-urinary infections.

Altogether there are over twenty different types of sexually transmitted infections. These include chlamydia, syphilis, genital herpes, genital warts and gonorrhoea.

How do you get infected?

An STI can only be caught through having sex with an infected partner. But sexually transmitted infections are very common and anyone who has sex can get infected. It isn't true that only people who have lots of partners get infected. Though obviously the more partners you have the more you put yourself at risk.

Can sexually transmitted infections be treated?

Most sexually transmitted infections can be treated quickly and easily, provided they are detected at an early stage. However, some of them can cause long-term problems, such as infertility in women, if they are not treated.

There is no known cure for the HIV virus (see pages 70–71).

How can you tell if you've got an STI?

Some sexually transmitted infections give you symptoms that show you that there is something wrong. However, many infections, including HIV, often give no signs, so the infection can remain undetected for years. So if you have had unprotected sex and think that you might have caught something it's very important to check to make sure you're not infected.

Symptoms that may indicate you have an STI are:

- ✖ an unusual discharge from the vagina or penis
- ✖ a burning sensation when you urinate or have sex
- ✖ spots or sores on the vagina or penis
- ✖ itchiness or rashes around the genital area
- ✖ warts on the vagina or penis.

How can I protect myself from STIs?

By being very choosy about who you have sex with, and by practising safer sex, you stand a pretty good chance of avoiding the infections altogether. Don't allow yourself to be pressurised into having unprotected sex.

Girls should have regular smear tests – every three years – as soon as they become sexually active, since they can reveal problems early on. Regular smear tests have also been proved to reduce greatly the chances of serious cervical cancer developing.

What to do if you think you have an STI

Don't ignore it! STIs don't go away by themselves and many can do you serious harm if they're not treated. Besides, if you don't sort things out, you'll be passing the STI on to whoever you sleep with – so you won't be very popular! There's nothing 'shameful' about catching an STI, and there's really no need to be embarrassed or worried what other people will think, so you should never be put off doing something about it.

What you need to do is find your nearest special STI clinic and get down there pronto. Once you're there, there's no need to feel ashamed or nervous because all the other patients are there for the same reason as you, and none of the doctors or nurses are going to be shocked or disgusted – they've seen it all before. STI clinics are usually friendly, helpful and discreet. You don't have to give your real name or any details about yourself if you don't want to, and no one else will ever know you've been there. You don't need an appointment or a referral from your GP (you don't even need to tell your GP you're going) and the whole thing is free. All in all, a visit to an STI clinic is not the big deal you might fear, so there is no excuse for not going.

You can find out where your nearest clinic is by looking up 'Sexually transmitted disease' or 'Venereal disease' in the telephone directory. Most large hospitals have a genito-urinary medicine (GUM) clinic.

Adapted from *Sex: How? Why? What? The Teenager's Guide* by Jane Goldman

Chlamydia

Chlamydia is the most common sexually transmitted infection in young people. Figures show that 10% of sexually active teenagers in the UK have chlamydia. The problem with chlamydia is that there are often no symptoms, so people do not know that they have the infection.

Chlamydia is caused by a bacteria and can easily be passed from one person to another, especially if they have sex without using a condom. However, if it is diagnosed early enough, it can be treated with a course of antibiotics, which will cure the infection in two weeks. Left untreated it can lead to pelvic inflammatory disease and infertility.

for your file

'Dear Lucy, I'm worried. I got drunk and had sex with someone I'd only just met. I think I may have caught a sexually transmitted infection. How can I tell? What should I do?' Sam

Write Lucy's reply to Sam.

69

You and your body – safer sex, STIs and AIDS

HIV and AIDS

AIDS The facts

What is AIDS?

AIDS stands for Acquired Immune Deficiency Syndrome, and it's a fatal disease – in other words, if you have it you will almost definitely die. Here are the facts about AIDS.

- AIDS is caused by a virus called HIV, which stands for Human Immunodeficiency Virus. People who are infected with this virus usually go on to develop AIDS.
- There is no cure for HIV or AIDS, and no vaccination that can protect you from them.
- You catch the HIV virus from other people who are infected with it.
- It's impossible to tell who has got it and who hasn't without having a blood test. That's because people infected with HIV don't seem ill, feel ill or look any different from anyone else until they start to develop AIDS. This can happen as long as ten years after getting infected.
- *Anyone* can get infected by the HIV virus. You don't have to be gay, a drug-user or anything else.
- People carry the HIV virus in their blood and other body fluids, like semen and vaginal juices.
- When you have sex, you and your partner come into contact with one another's fluids. If one of you has HIV, the other could get infected.
- The only way to help protect yourself and your partner is to use a condom when you have sex.

Is it easy to catch HIV?

If you're not having sex, there's hardly any risk:

- You can't catch HIV by touching an infected person, holding hands with them or hugging them.
- You can't catch the virus from using things an infected person has used (like phones, headphones, books, soap or towels), sitting where they've sat (including on toilets), wearing clothes they've worn, using the same shower or swimming pool or sharing things like food, knives and forks, plates, cups and make-up.
- You can't catch the virus from an infected person breathing, sneezing or coughing near you.

So you can only catch it from having sex?

Well, no. You catch the HIV virus when an infected person's body fluids enter your body, and there are ways this can happen that don't involve sex. The good news is that these risks are quite easily avoided:

- If an infected person was bleeding and you also happened to have an open wound – even a scratch or a small cut – there would be a chance that some of their blood could enter your bloodstream if you touched them. If someone is bleeding, be careful.

> If you have to clean up someone else's blood, always wear rubber gloves to protect yourself.

- If you're a drug-user who injects drugs and you share a needle with an infected person, you would run a very high risk of getting infected. Even if you cleaned the needle first, some of their blood would still be there, and it would go directly into your bloodstream. The only way a drug-user can stay safe is always to use a fresh needle and syringe.

> If you ever find a syringe or needle lying around, don't touch it – it could be infected.

- Anything that has had blood on it is a potential hazard. If you are considering having a tattoo, acupuncture or electrolysis, or getting your ears pierced, you should always check that the equipment has been properly sterilised before it is used on you.

> It's not a good idea to share a toothbrush or wet-shave razor with anyone, because of the risk of blood from bleeding gums or shaving cuts.

How can you tell if you are infected with HIV?

There are no immediate symptoms, so the only way to tell is by having a blood test. If a person is infected with HIV, their body produces antibodies, which can be detected by an HIV test. But it takes around three to four months after a person contracts HIV before a test will show a positive result.

This is not really an AIDS test, because it tests for antibodies to the virus, and it may be a long time before someone who is HIV positive develops the symptoms of AIDS, if at all. HIV tests can be carried out free and in confidence at your local genito-urinary clinic.

Adapted from *Sex: How? Why? What? The Teenager's Guide* by Jane Goldman

In groups

1 Discuss what you have learned from the article 'AIDS – the facts' on page 70. What is the HIV virus? How can it be transmitted? Who is at risk? What precautions should you take to avoid becoming infected?

2 Draw up a test-yourself quiz consisting of statements about AIDS, some of which are true and some of which are false. Then give your quiz to another group to do.

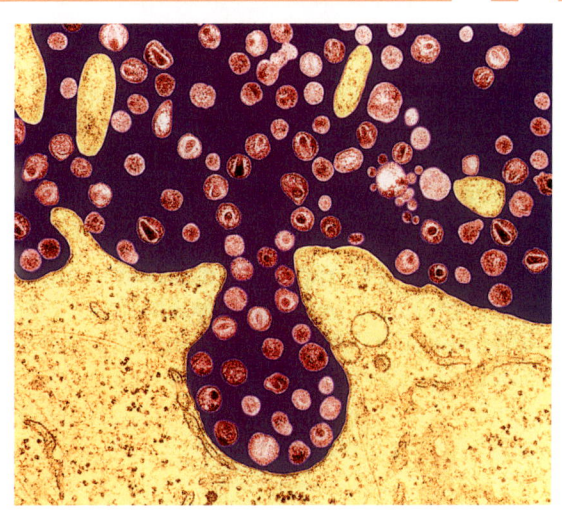

for your file

Design a page for an internet website which aims to give teenagers essential information about AIDS.

A microscopic view of the HIV virus

Attitudes to sex

Young people have widely differing views about sex and AIDS, as these comments show.

❝ I think sex before marriage is wrong. If people wait until they are married and stick to one partner, then the AIDS problem would be solved. It only exists because people don't behave responsibly and sleep around. ❞

❝ I don't see anything wrong with experimenting while you're young and having lots of partners. AIDS doesn't bother me. Why should it? ❞

❝ Of course I'm concerned about AIDS, but I'm not going to let it stand in the way of my having sex. But that doesn't mean I intend to jump into bed with someone at the first opportunity. I think it's important to develop a relationship first. ❞

❝ People, boys especially, need to learn to be sensible and responsible about sex. Too many people I know take unnecessary risks. If you're going to have sex with someone you need to care for them and that involves thinking about all the possible consequences of having sex. ❞

❝ Adults keep on and on about the risks of having sex, but I think they're exaggerating. It's just a matter of luck whether you catch an infection or get yourself pregnant. ❞

Teenagers think HIV is 'irrelevant'

Teenagers think that HIV is 'nothing to do with them', according to a health education survey published to mark World Aids Day.

The study of 16–18-year-olds found that the majority saw the virus as 'irrelevant to people their age'. Most knew about its effects and how it was transmitted but were still unlikely to use a condom.

The teenagers saw Aids as an issue to concern 'promiscuous older people' and saw condoms as an 'inconvenience'.

The latest figures show 30,000 people are HIV positive in Britain, with 10,000 of them unaware that they are infected. Worldwide 34 million people have the infection.

From *The Guardian*, 1 December 1999

In groups

1 Read the quotes in the section 'Attitudes to sex', then discuss the comments that the young people make. What is your attitude towards sex, relationships and marriage?

2 What is your attitude towards AIDS? Do you see it as 'irrelevant', as the teenagers in the survey did?

Share your views with those of other groups in a class discussion.

16 You as a citizen –

Globalisation In the 21st century it is important to see yourself not only as a UK citizen, but as a citizen of Europe and of the world. This unit examines some key global issues and how they affect everybody.

One of the most important developments in recent years has been the spread of globalisation. Globalisation is the term used to describe the process whereby people, governments and businesses throughout the world are becoming increasingly dependent on one another.

What are the causes of globalisation?

One of the main causes of globalisation has been the development of huge transnational corporations (see box) whose businesses operate in many different countries. This development has accelerated in recent years following the collapse of communism and the spread of the free market across the world.

Another cause of globalisation has been the technological revolution that began in the latter half of the 20th century. Developments in transport mean that people and goods can be moved swiftly from one part of the world to another. Developments in communication mean that information can be sent across the world in seconds via the internet, e-mail, fax and telephone.

Transnational corporations (TNCs)

Transnationals (sometimes called multinationals) are major business corporations which have subsidiaries, investments or operations in more than one country. According to the United Nations, TNCs are associations which 'possess and control means of production or services outside the country in which they were established'. Some TNCs are viewed as threats to national sovereignty, exerting undue influence to achieve their corporate goals or sacrificing human and environmental well-being in order to maximise profits. Annual sales of some TNCs exceed $100 billion, far greater than the exports and imports of most Third World nations.

TNCs include:
- Media corporations, for example, **News International**
- Computer companies, for example, **Microsoft**
- Oil companies, for example, **Royal Dutch/Shell, Exxon**
- Motor companies, for example, **Ford, Toyota**
- Supermarket corporations, for example, **Wal-Mart Stores Inc**.

• A global village •

It is sometimes said that we now live in a global village, since it is possible to live and work in another country, and still keep in touch with friends and family on the other side of the world, in the way that you would if you lived in a village. More and more people have jobs which involve either commuting from one country to another on a regular basis, or living abroad for a while.

In groups

Globalisation – what do you think?

"Globalisation is a good thing, because the more people come to see themselves as citizens of the world, the less conflicts there are likely to be."

"It gives too much power to transnational corporations whose decisions can influence world trade as much as the decisions of governments, but they are not accountable to anybody except their shareholders."

"In one sense, it's a good idea for countries to be inter-dependent. In another, it's dangerous. A crisis in one country could easily lead to problems in others. Globalisation has its disadvantages as well as its advantages."

In groups, discuss what you understand by the term 'globalisation'. What are the main causes of globalisation? What do you think the effects of globalisation will be? Do you view it as a good thing or a bad thing? Explain why.

of the world

The internet

One of the major driving forces behind globalisation has been the development of the internet. The internet enables information to be exchanged with speed and ease across the world.

The communications revolution brought about by the internet has affected people's lives worldwide. However, due to the availability and cost of computer technology, the impact so far has been much greater in developed countries than in developing countries.

In groups

What impact has the development of the internet had across the world? How do you think its development will affect people's lives in the future?

The information superhighway

The establishment of world-wide networks linking computers has caused an enormously important turnaround in the access to and exchange of information. With more than 40 million users and exponential growth, the Internet has become an irreplaceable tool. Immediate access to databases and sources of information, the possibility of making links through electronic mail and news groups has made it more possible for groups to side-step the one-way flow of information imposed by the big news agencies. Thousands of non-governmental organisations, civil associations, and other groups have opened new routes for rapid, reliable and reasonably-priced communication. Citizens in different parts of the world have made their voices heard together, supporting diverse causes, while at the same time making their knowledge available to others.

This capacity to link up networks convinced many people that the democratization of access to sources of information is now an indisputable and irreversible fact. However, this development also has its flaws.

Due to the high levels of standardisation needed for such networks to function, languages which use non-Roman characters, used by people with little economic clout, have had serious difficulties in joining the tide of world information. Be that as it may, it is still possible to find programmes with Arabic, Chinese, Hebrew, Cyrillic and other characters. But English remains the doorway to the 'information superhighway'. Most of the servers putting information at the disposal of network users, like the Internet, are in the developed countries, particularly in the United States.

From *The World Guide* 1999/2000

Problems of the internet

The internet revolution has brought a number of problems.

Some of the issues are concerned with freedom of access to information. Governments are concerned about security and fear that the internet could be used to spread information that will threaten national security. There is also the problem of pornographic material and how to prevent it being accessible to children. A third issue concerns copyright. How can an author prevent someone from copying their work onto the internet anonymously or even claiming it to be their own?

Currently there is considerable debate about whether or not the internet should be censored. Some people think that censorship laws should be introduced to prevent libel and to control material that is either pornographic or racist. Others argue that all information should be freely available and that to censor it in any way would be an infringement of people's civil liberties.

In groups

1 Discuss the problems that there are with the internet. What other problems can arise?

2 Do you think information on the internet should be censored in any way? What are the arguments for and against censorship of the internet?

for your file

Write an article about the internet, explaining its impact, commenting on its problems and saying how you think it will affect people's lives in the future.

You as a citizen – of the world

Global warming

Global warming is the term used to describe the increase in the average world temperatures brought about by human activities. It is seen by many scientists as the most serious threat to the world's environment.

The greenhouse effect

Global warming is caused by what is known as the greenhouse effect. This is the name given to the process in which certain gases in the lower atmosphere allow the sun's rays through to heat the surface of the Earth, then trap a proportion of the heat as it is radiated back into space. It is called the greenhouse effect because the gases in the atmosphere are acting like the panes of glass in a greenhouse to trap the heat.

Without the greenhouse effect the Earth would be unable to support life, because the temperature on the surface would be too low. During the last 100 years, however, human activities have altered the levels of some of the greenhouse gases in the atmosphere. This has caused global warming.

In groups

Discuss what you learn from this page about global warming. What is the greenhouse effect? What human activities have increased the greenhouse effect? What are the effects of global warming?

From *Global Warming*, Young People's Trust for the Environment and Nature Conservation

Greenhouse gases

Carbon dioxide (CO_2) is one of the main greenhouse gases. The level of CO_2 in the atmosphere has increased by nearly 30% since pre-industrial times.

One reason for the increase is deforestation. Forests affect the amount of CO_2 in the atmosphere because trees take in CO_2 from the air as they grow. When forests are cleared and burned, there are fewer trees to take in the CO_2. As the world's forests are destroyed to provide land for the landless poor or for commercial logging, nearly 2 billion tonnes of CO_2 are released into the atmosphere each year through forest burning.

But the main source of CO_2 from human activity is through the burning of fossil fuels to provide energy in power stations, factories and motor vehicles. The countries mainly responsible for the production of CO_2 are the industrialised countries of the developed world.

Other gases which contribute to the greenhouse effect are:

- **methane**, which is released into the atmosphere by agricultural activities, waste disposal and during coal-mining and oil exploration;
- **nitrous oxide**, which is a by-product of industrial and agricultural processes, such as the use of nitrogenous fertilisers;
- **chlorofluorocarbons** (CFCs), found widely in fridges, air conditioners and aerosols, until limits were imposed on their production to protect the Earth's ozone layer.

••• [The effects of global warming] •••

If no action is taken the greenhouse effect could lead to a rise in average global temperatures of between 1.5–4.5 degrees C as early as the year 2030. The effects are already showing – the ten hottest years since the 1860s have all been during the 1980s and 1990s.

- **Storms** – storms and hurricanes will become more frequent and stronger as oceans heat up, causing more water to evaporate.
- **Droughts** – continental heartlands will dry out more in summer.
- **Floods** – there will be increased flooding in coastal areas and river estuaries such as Bangladesh and the Nile Delta; London and many other British coastal cities will be threatened also.

From *The A–Z of World Development*

How can we reduce global warming?

Limiting the use of fossil fuels to reduce CO_2 levels will cost an estimated $350 billion over the next 10 years. Irrespective of the costs, the global community cannot agree on the specific measures to reduce or switch to less polluting forms of energy. Most effort has been spent on cutting CO_2 emissions. Yet proposals for a 20% reduction in emissions by 2005 were vetoed by the United States, the former Soviet Union, Japan and the United Kingdom – countries which between them account for half of global emissions.

Extensive tree plantations, acting as 'carbon sinks', have been proposed as one solution to absorbing the 5 billion tonnes of carbon generated each year. Other proposals include growing algae or issuing 'carbon permits'. Algae, grown in either fresh or saline water, are ten times more efficient at CO_2 uptake than trees. Another proposal is for the allocation of 'carbon permits' to individual countries based on their population size. Countries wishing to exceed their permitted level of carbon emissions would have to acquire permits from other countries to cover the excess production.

Slow the global warming

It is important to slow the warming as much as possible. This means using less fossil fuel, eliminating CFCs altogether, and slowing down deforestation. This can be achieved best through:

- **energy conservation**, including better use of public transport and cleaner, more efficient cars;
- **energy efficiency**, by greater use of gas which produces less CO_2 than coal and oil, and through renewable energy such as solar power;
- **stopping the destruction of rain forests** (deforestation) and starting to replace trees (afforestation) to soak up carbon dioxide.

A United Nations panel has estimated that we need to reduce global fuel use by 60% immediately in order to stabilise the climate. Current commitments by those governments participating in CO_2 reduction will only lower global CO_2 by 4–6%. Although the developed industrialised nations still produce most CO_2, the rapidly developing nations of South America and Asia are increasing their CO_2 production at a much higher rate, and by 2010 they will overtake the West as the main producers of CO_2.

The developing countries are reluctant to participate in any CO_2 emission reduction plans, arguing that they did not create global warming and that it is the responsibility of developed countries to cut their own emissions.

From *Global Warming*, Young People's Trust for the Environment and Nature Conservation

An energy policy for the 21st century

In developing an energy policy for the 21st century we need to look at ways of meeting our energy needs that are economic, efficient and will not damage the environment.

We need to promote energy conservation, by improving the efficiency of current methods of energy production and lessening the environmental damage they cause.

At the same time, we need to develop renewable energy resources, such as wind power, water power and solar power, so that we depend less and less on energy from fossil fuels.

In groups

1 Discuss what **governments** can do to reduce CO_2 emissions and cut down global warming. Why is it difficult to get international agreement on this issue?

2 Discuss what **businesses and institutions** such as schools can do to use energy more efficiently. Carry out a survey to find out how efficiently energy is being used in your school buildings. Look at such factors as insulation, the energy efficiency of electrical goods, whether lights and appliances are left running unnecessarily and building design. Draft a report, based on your findings, making suggestions as to how the school could save energy.

3 Discuss what **individuals** can do to change their energy habits and reduce their energy use, for example, alter how they use transport, support recycling schemes. Talk about how these actions would save energy. What other ways of conserving energy can you suggest?

for your file

Write a letter to a newspaper saying why you are concerned about global warming and what you think needs to be done about it.

You as a citizen – of the world

Keeping the peace

The United Nations (UN) was set up in 1945 after the end of the Second World War. It is an association of countries which aims to promote international peace, security and co-operation.

The UN Security Council

The Security Council is the UN body responsible for debating and taking decisions on conflict situations. It has five permanent members: China, France, Russia, the United Kingdom and the USA. The other ten members are elected for two years. The five permanent members have the power to veto any decisions they don't agree with.

Because the UN Security could not agree to take military action against Iraq in 2003, the US-led coalition, which included Britain, decided to take action without waiting for UN approval.

A shattered dream

The UN's founding charter proclaimed its mission to save 'succeeding generations from the scourge of war'. It would tackle global poverty to bring about higher standards of living everywhere. The UN system was supposed to 'harmonise the actions of nations', preventing the clashes which had led to two world wars.

After 50 difficult years, and despite some significant achievements, it faces a grim reality. Local wars are widespread. Though living standards have improved in parts of the world, tens of millions still starve or die young. Most damagingly, the vision of an *international* body which could sort out arguments between *nations* has not been realised.

From *The Guardian*, 27 June 1995

Why has the UN failed to bring peace?

For over 40 years the UN's attempts to maintain international peace and security was hampered by the cold war, during which its members divided into communist and Western power blocs with conflicting political interests. The power of the veto in the Security Council meant that when conflicts occurred the UN could not agree on what action to take. For example, the UN did not intervene when the USSR invaded Hungary in 1956 and sent troops into Afghanistan in 1979. Between 1965 and 1975 over two million Vietnamese and 58,000 US soldiers died in the Vietnam war. But the UN never even debated the war.

When the communist bloc collapsed in 1989–90 it was hoped that a new era would begin, in which the UN would be able to play a more active role in the promotion of peace. The Gulf War, which followed Iraq's invasion of Kuwait in 1990, showed that the UN could act against an aggressor when member states agreed. However, many of the peacekeeping attempts by the UN during the 1990s ended in failure.

While the UN has been active in sending peacekeeping troops into conflict areas, it has stopped short of giving them the authority to take the decisive action necessary to be effective. Examples of UN failures in the 1990s were in Rwanda, where UN troops did not intervene during the massacre of thousands of people by the government and its supporters, and in Bosnia, where the UN troops were initially ineffective, as both sides repeatedly broke ceasefires negotiated by the UN.

Critics argue that the UN will continue to be ineffective until it is prepared to commit its troops to take firmer military action, even if this means UN troops getting more involved in conflicts than they have done in the past.

In groups

Discuss what you have learned from the information on this page about how the UN has attempted to bring peace to the world and why so far it has failed.

The arms trade

Many of the wars that have taken place since 1945 have been in the developing world. The arms that have been used in them have mostly come from the developed world.

ARMS TRADE FACTS

- Developing countries spend $2 billion a year on arms.
- More than 90% of the weapons traded come from six countries, four of which are members of the UN Security Council.

The UK and the arms trade

❝ The UK is one of the world's top arms dealers exporting $5 billion of weapons annually to over 140 countries … and yet in 1998 the arms trade accounted for just 2.7% of the UK's visible exports and only around 0.5% of the country's jobs. There is no reason, either economic or ethical, for the arms trade to exist. ❞
Campaign Against Arms Trade leaflet

❝ It is difficult to imagine any other British industry which could cause death and injury on a large scale and remain not merely unaccountable but receive large sums of taxpayers' money in export credit guarantees. ❞ from an Oxfam report, *Small Arms, Wrong Hands*

❝ Aid donors like Britain are quick to chide the poor for spending too much on arms – yet they are slow to apply the same standards to our own military budgets or to the way we train and sell arms to those very same countries. ❞ World Development Movement leaflet

ARMS EXPORTS

… FUEL WARS
Millions of people have been killed in wars since 1945. Most of these wars, which make the world a more dangerous place for us all, have been fought with imported arms.

… WASTE RESOURCES
The purchase and production of arms wastes resources, diverting finance, skills and materials that could be used to ensure that everyone has food, clean water, housing, health care and education.

… SUPPORT REPRESSIVE REGIMES
British arms are often sold to governments, like that of Indonesia, which have appalling human rights records. Such sales legitimise these regimes and further demoralise their peoples.

CAMPAIGN AGAINST ARMS TRADE

An ethical foreign policy

In 1997 the foreign secretary, Robin Cook, announced an ethical foreign policy, which would ban the sale of arms to dictators or to countries where arms might be used aggressively. However, since 1997 arms have been sold to 20 countries engaged in serious conflicts.

In groups

'It's all very well to suggest that the UK shouldn't manufacture and sell arms, but why should we stop doing so and sacrifice British jobs? Unless all countries agree to do so – and there's no hope of that – we'd only be punishing ourselves.'

'Someone somewhere has got to do something that will stop the senseless slaughter. Britain should show the way and stop exporting arms to anyone anywhere.'

Discuss these views of the arms trade.

for your file

Write your views on the arms trade and the part Britain plays in it.

17 You and the community –

Pressure groups

How much say do you have in what happens to you?

If we want to show that we think those who govern us have done something wrong or are about to make the wrong decision, we have to make a protest of some kind. Individually what we can do is take the matter up with our MP or the local council. But if it's an important issue, there may be a pressure group that we can join.

A pressure group is a group of people who try to influence the local or national government to change their policy by mounting a publicity campaign to get their point across. The aim of a campaign is to bring the facts about the issue to the attention of as many people as possible, putting forward the reasons why the people in power have made the wrong decision. If enough protesters make their objections clear, the decision might be altered.

In groups

What issues do you feel so strongly about that you would be prepared to campaign for them?

Think about:

changes to the appearance of the area where you live – knocking down an attractive part of town, building a motorway through peaceful countryside;

changes to the facilities of your area – closing down a swimming pool or youth centre, building on a football pitch;

changes to the safety of your area – a refusal by the council to improve street lighting near an alleyway, or to put a 30mph speed restriction on the main road through a village;

things which you think are wrong – hunting, trials of GM crops.

Each group should decide on an issue that you would be prepared to campaign about. Then share your views in a class discussion.

In groups

Discuss the different techniques that pressure groups use. What is your view of non-violent civil disobedience? Can it be justified or should pressure groups always work within the law?

Pressure group techniques

Pressure groups use a variety of techniques to achieve their aims. These are generally lawful, but some groups choose to break the law to promote their cause.

Lawful pressure

Pressure groups sometimes contact politicians by sending a deputation to meet MPs and to put their case. They often try to gain coverage in the media, to argue their point of view. This can be done in many ways, for example by adverts, press releases and media stunts.

One favourite media stunt that pressure groups like to use is to dedicate a particular day or week to a specific cause.

Unlawful pressure

Sometimes pressure groups use civil disobedience to promote their cause. This is when a person chooses to break the law in a non-violent way, for example, when a person chains themselves to a tree as a protest about it being cut down to make way for a new road.

A few pressure groups break the law by violent protest. One example is the Animal Liberation Front, which has attacked and fire-bombed laboratories involved in animal experiments.

Adapted from *Democracy in Action* by Simon Foster

pressure groups and campaigning

The Pedestrians Association

Each year 60,000 pedestrians are killed or injured on Britain's roads. The Pedestrians Association campaigns to make walking safer, more convenient and easier.

Every day as a pedestrian you are likely to encounter certain hazards. The Pedestrians Association suggests what action you should take.

Building site obstructions
These hazards take many forms: scaffolding, skips and mounds of building materials. They must be licensed and lit. Check with your local council that they are.

Holes in the pavement
Holes are made by the utility companies (gas, electricity, water, telephone or cable). It is required that such holes should be fenced and lit, and when the work is finished, the pavement should be restored to its previous standard. Complaints should be addressed to the utility concerned or to the council.

The same applies to access covers, which may be broken or sticking up.

Dog dirt
Local bylaws sometimes make fouling of the footway by dogs an offence. If you have such bylaws and dog owners ignore them, press your local council for enforcement.

Damaged pavements
The local authority maintains most highways. If you trip and fall over a pavement slab that's sticking up an inch (25cm) or more you may have a good case for compensation.

Pavement parking
There is still no national ban on pavement parking, but you can complain to the police, especially if vehicles parked on the pavement are causing an obstruction.

Pavement cycling
This is becoming such a common practice that many people don't seem to realise it's illegal. But it is an offence. Ask your local police to step up enforcement with their powers of a £20 on the spot fine.

No pavement?
This doesn't let the council off the hook. If there isn't a pavement, ask for one. Highway authorities have a duty to provide one where they consider it's necessary and desirable.

Pedestrian crossings
If there is no crossing where you think there should be one, or if the 'green man' time is too short to allow you to cross in safety, tell your local council.

Too fast?
Where conditions are unsafe for pedestrians because of traffic speeds, remind your local council it has powers to regulate traffic on non-trunk roads and urge the police to improve enforcement of existing regulations.

It's time to put your foot **down**

From *It's Time to Put Your Foot Down*, Pedestrians Association

In groups

Discuss the hazards that pedestrians can encounter and the advice on what you should do if you encounter such hazards. What particular hazards are there for pedestrians in the area where you live?

You and the community – pressure groups and campaigning

Organising a campaign to make your area safer

What campaign?

Discuss what problems there are with traffic in your area. Identify what you consider to be the main problem, and suggest what could be done about it.

Form yourselves into an action group and work together to plan a campaign to publicise the problem and to put pressure on the appropriate authorities to do something about it.

Give your action group a name

This must be a catchy name or a set of initials. For example, if you live in South Mimms, you could be SMASH – South Mimms Action on Safety Hazards. Or if you come from Haslemere, you could be HARM – Haslemere Action on Road Menace. Or you could simply call yourself after your class – the 9N Traffic Action Group, for example.

Surveying opinions and collecting information

You've decided there's a problem and what you think should be done about it, but does anyone else agree?

Find out who in the neighbourhood agrees with you by contacting the local community centre and sending someone to talk to any neighbourhood groups, for example, your local residents' or tenants' group or neighbourhood association.

Circulate a leaflet or a short questionnaire to ask local people how they feel about the issue. Ask them to express their views on what needs to be done to see if they have any alternative suggestions. Remember to get the views of some local businesses and shopkeepers as well as those of local residents.

Planning your campaign

Hold a planning meeting to discuss what you have learned from your survey of opinions about support for your campaign. Study the list (below) of things you could do as part of your campaign and decide which ones you are going to do:

● Produce posters to put up locally ● Design and distribute a newsletter ● Organise a petition ● Produce a press release ● Organise a media event ● Send a deputation to the local council ● Write to the local MP

Producing your own newsletter

Use your ICT skills to design and produce a newsletter explaining what the purpose of the action group is and saying what your plans are.

Follow these guidelines to help to get your message across:

- Design a heading which includes the group's name and the school's address.
- Keep it short (two sides of A4 maximum) and break up the text with bold, eye-catching headlines.
- Don't assume that everyone will be aware of the problem (or that they will see it your way).
- Include drawings, cartoons, diagrams or photos.
- Make sure there is a contact name and address.

Contacting the council

Send a copy of your newsletter to your local councillor along with a letter inviting them to come to the school to discuss the issue with you and the rest of your class.

Hitting the headlines

To win your campaign you must get the public on your side. And there's no better way of reaching people than through the media. A story in the papers or on the radio will be read or heard by thousands of people.

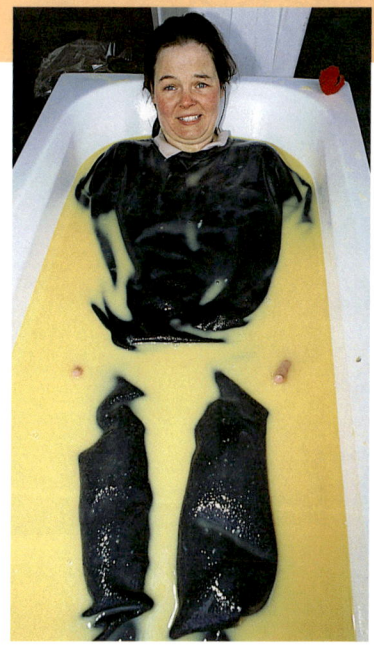

Here's how to use your local media to get results:

- **Give your story an 'angle'.** Local papers are keen to write about something that is affecting local people.

- **Invite the local press** to attend any presentation you make by sending, or faxing, a press release to the news editor. Fax your press release to the picture desk too. But have someone ready to take your own photos too – in case the professionals are too busy to be able to come.

- **Organise a stunt** – anything that would make an interesting photo or radio story. You could cycle in gas masks to draw attention to air pollution or dress up as green men to publicise the need for a new pedestrian crossing.

- **Involve your MP.** Present your survey results or petition to your local MP in person – send local newspapers a press release and invite them to photograph the occasion. If your MP supports your views, they may be happy to pose with you.

How to write a good press release

- Keep it short (just one side of A4 paper) and to the point.
- Put the information about the date, time and place in bold type.
- Get the most important information into the first couple of attention-grabbing sentences — who, what, where, when and why.
- Include a quote which sums up your campaign's message. The paper can print it to save themselves the trouble of interviewing you.
- If there's a lot of detail to include, put it in notes at the end.
- Give a contact name and phone number at the bottom in case the journalist wants to follow up the story.

= PRESS RELEASE =

Photocall: Saturday 11th March 2001 11.30am Newtown Town Hall

On Saturday 11th March the N.Y.A.T.F. (Newtown Youth Against Traffic Fumes) group from Sir Albert Graham School will present their petition **STOP POLLUTING OUR STREETS** to local MP Janice Buttersworth at the Town Hall.

The petition is in protest at the problem of traffic fumes and gives suggestions of what needs to be done to clean up air quality.

'Nine out of ten local people want the council to reduce the amount of traffic in town,' explains Kylie Challenger, one of the campaign organisers. 'That means banning through traffic from the town centre in the daytime, a better, cheaper bus service and more cycle lanes.'

For more information about N.Y.A.T.F. and its campaign, contact Kylie Challenger or William Powers at Sir Albert Graham School, South Lane, Newtown NT1 6TT.
School telephone no.: 01308 12346.

Adapted from Causing a Stink! The Eco Warrior's Handbook by Caroline Clayton

In groups

Study the press release and the helpful hints (left), then draft a press release about your campaign.

for your file

In groups discuss what you have learned about how to run a campaign from the information and activities on these pages. Draw up a list of advice – 'Our Top Ten Tips on How to Run a Campaign'. Then each put a copy of the list in your files, together with a short written statement saying what went well during your campaign, what you've learned from running it and what you would do differently in running another campaign in the future.

18 You and other people –

What is mental illness?

Mental illness – Some questions and answers

What is mental illness?

Mental illness is the term used to describe an illness which affects the mind rather than the body. Many different mental illnesses can affect your mind, just as there are many different physical illnesses which can affect your body.

Mental illnesses often involve feelings of depression, anxiety and confusion. Most people experience such feelings from time to time, particularly after a distressing event or during a period of stress. A person suffering from a mental illness experiences these feelings so strongly or over such a long period of time that they find it very hard to cope with everyday life.

What is a nervous breakdown?

Because it can be difficult to describe mental illness exactly, we sometimes say that a person has had a nervous breakdown. We use it to cover a wide range of mental states that make it difficult for a person to cope with life. However, because it doesn't describe a specific mental illness, it's not a term that is used by psychiatrists or psychologists.

How common is mental illness?

Mental illness affects at least 15 people in every 100 at some stage of their lives. So it is likely that at some point you will have a friend or relative that becomes mentally ill.

Can mental illness be cured?

Mental illness is often a temporary condition. It can be treated successfully, though there is the possibility that it may re-occur. Some mental illnesses can be cured through talking treatments, either individual sessions with a psychiatrist or psychotherapist, or group sessions in which experiences are shared. Other illnesses may require a course of drugs as well.

Are people who are mentally ill dangerous?

A small minority of mentally ill people may become violent and aggressive unless they are treated, but most of them are not dangerous. They are far more likely to hurt themselves than other people.

Why are people so afraid of mental illness?

One reason is that people seem to think they will be regarded as weak if they are mentally ill. But anyone can become mentally ill. It's nothing to be ashamed of.

⊕ In groups

1 Sometimes people with mental illnesses are referred to as 'loonies', 'nutters' or 'crackpots'. Some people argue that we should stop using such terms because by doing so we are discriminating against people who are mentally ill. Others argue that such terms are harmless. What do you think?

2 People who are mentally ill are often the victims of prejudice. Discuss what forms this prejudice takes. Suggest what a) individuals, b) the media, c) the government could do to help change people's attitudes.

Adapted from 'Caring for the mentally ill', *Issues 3*

people with mental illnesses

Mental illness in the family

How can you help someone in your family who is mentally ill? The way you can help most is by accepting that they are ill, giving sympathy and support and ensuring that they get professional help.

In groups

Discuss what you learn from this page about how a family member may behave if they have a mental illness, and the feelings a young person may experience in such circumstances.

Mental health problems

A lot of people find it hard to cope at times. This may be because a friend or relative has died; there may be job worries or money problems; friendships or relationships may have ended unhappily.

When things like this happen, many people naturally feel sad or depressed, alone or angry. Sometimes they may show how they feel by being rude or grumpy, or by wanting to be alone a lot, or to go out all the time. These are usually ordinary reactions to uncomfortable feelings and upsetting events in life which we may all experience.

However, some people's reactions may become more disturbing. If, for example:

1 your mother or father refuses to leave her or his room for a long period of time, is unable to make the effort to get washed and dressed, and maybe shouts angrily for most of the day; or

2 your brother or sister thinks that voices are telling him or her what to do and is bewildered and afraid,

then it could be that he or she is suffering from a serious mental health problem.

Some types of mental illness

Manic-depressive illness causes extreme changes in mood from high spirits and over-activity to deep depression and lethargy; it often causes irritability that can be very wearing for the family. When someone is over excited he or she may spend all their money on, say, expensive presents, so that there is nothing left for the rent or clothes or food. When the person is feeling low and depressed, he or she may cry a lot, want to sleep all the time, or just stay in bed and be incapable of looking after the family and the household, and carrying on with their usual work.

Schizophrenia causes a great deal of distress and confusion in people's minds. It can lead to a person hearing voices, telling him or her what to do and producing strong feelings of confusion, bewilderment and fear; and it can cause him or her to think that all his or her thoughts are being controlled by others.

There are other types of mental illness, for example, **dementia** in old people, when some grandparents may become very forgetful and confused, and their behaviour becomes unpredictable. Some people suffer from **obsessive compulsive disorder** when, for example, they may feel that they have to keep things extremely clean and tidy or they become very anxious. Some sufferers may try to persuade everyone else to help with their rituals of cleaning.

How does this make you feel?

If your mum or dad or favourite aunt or uncle has become, during this time, a very different person, it may seem that no one is there to look after you, to listen to your worries or problems, or to help you with your feelings, too. You may feel scared, unsure and angry, sad or lonely. You may be ashamed or embarrassed and not understand what is happening. Maybe you don't want anyone else to know. You may even have worries about your own mental health – that you have, or will have, the same problem as your mum or dad. You may even feel angry with them for making you feel so frightened and confused.

It will always help to talk to someone else, and to find an adult who can understand. They may be able to reassure you and help you to get the right support from a doctor or a social worker.

But remember, it is not your responsibility to make them well – there is a limit to how far you can help them. Most people who suffer from periods of mental illness need professional help, arranged through their GP, and they can improve with therapy and medication.

From Mental Health Problems – What Do They Mean?

You and other people – people with mental illnesses

The causes of mental illness

Mental illness is usually the result of a combination of factors. The article below discusses the various causes of mental illness.

What are the causes of mental illness?

PHYSICAL CAUSES

Illness and accidents

Often physical illnesses leave a person feeling very low and depressed. This can happen after a bad attack of 'flu and is quite common after an operation. As they grow older some people suffer from illnesses which affect their brain. This is known as dementia. A person with severe dementia can become very confused and unable to recognise people and objects.

An accident in which a person suffers a severe head injury can cause brain damage and mental illness.

Toxic states

Some people poison themselves over the course of several years through drinking alcohol to excess or through taking drugs. These substances may damage the brain and produce serious mental illness. Studies of the effects of ecstasy have shown that the drug decreases levels of the neurotransmitter serotonin in the brain and damages nerve endings. Lowered serotonin levels have been linked to an increased risk of depression and dementia in later life.

Inherited features

We are all different, but each of us inherits certain features from our parents. How far a person's own body chemistry makes him more or less likely to develop a mental illness is difficult to say. People from families in which mental illness has occurred before are more likely to become ill than other people. But is this because of the way they are made or because of the strain of having someone who has been mentally ill in the family?

SOCIAL CAUSES

Family pressures

One of the commonest causes of mental illness is strain in the home. People who have unsettled and insecure childhoods are more likely to have mental illnesses in later life. Adults who become depressed are often living under a strain at home. There may be relationship problems over money or sex, or a person may be overworking, while their partner feels neglected and lonely.

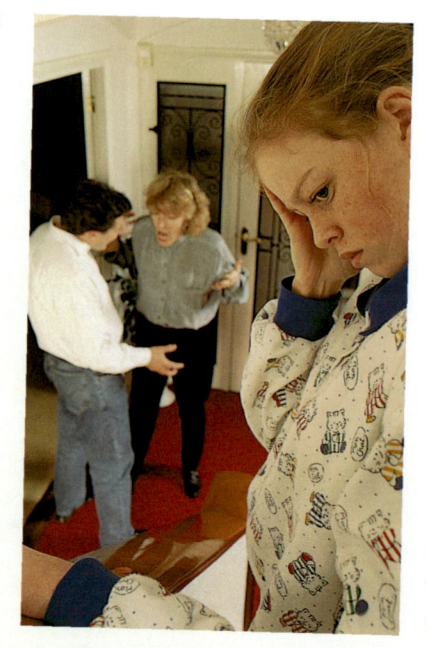

Group pressures

There are sometimes pressures on young people from parents, teachers or other teenagers. For example, a father may put pressure on his son to act 'like a real man' and to be 'rough and tough'. Some young people may feel very upset and become withdrawn, because they cannot, or do not want to, fit the pattern that is expected of them.

There are also many outside pressures on the individual, which may produce unhappiness and mental illness. Success in our society often tends to be measured in terms of money and possessions. A person who doesn't do well in exams or get on in their career may feel a failure and start to hate himself or herself.

ENVIRONMENTAL CAUSES

Living conditions

There are more mentally ill people living in big cities than in small towns and the countryside. One reason is that city life can be both stressful and lonely. Another reason is that a person with a serious mental illness is less obtrusive in a large city than in a small town or village. They may find it easier to blend into inner cities where eccentricities are often tolerated or simply ignored. Cities throughout the world have sections where people with odd behaviour tend to congregate. These are often the poorest areas where poor housing and overcrowding add to their difficulties.

Poor housing and overcrowding can put great pressures on a family. 'I've only got one room. There isn't anywhere for my little boy to play.'

Working conditions

People who have demanding jobs and who have to work long hours are living under stress. The worries and pressures can prove too much for them. Insecure people may feel the need to try to prove their worth to themselves and to the world by taking on jobs which are too exacting.

Nowadays many people often live a long way from the place where they work. People can spend over two hours a day just travelling to work and back, making stressful journeys during the rush hour. They may be so exhausted by the time they get home that they find it hard to be a wife and mother, or a husband and father.

Unemployment

Many people worry about losing their jobs. Being out of work can be far worse for one's mental health than being in a boring job. Even boring jobs have their rewards in terms of bringing you into contact with other people and making a person feel more valued than if they were doing nothing. Suicide rates always climb at times of high unemployment, and fall at times of full employment, such as in wartime.

⊕ In groups

1 Discuss what you learn from this article about the causes of mental illness. Which do you think are the most important causes?

2 Study a number of teenage magazines. Discuss the values that they are putting across and how they put pressure on their readers.

How else does society put pressure on people to behave in certain ways acording to their age and sex? What pressure do you feel under to behave in particular ways?

ODD OR ILL?

It is often difficult to draw the line between behaviour that is simply odd and eccentric and behaviour that is a sign of mental illness. The old lady who lives alone and talks to her cats as if they were people and then leaves all her money to them in her will – is she just eccentric or is she ill? What about the people you sometimes see in the street carrying placards because they feel they have an important message for all of us?

When you think about it, there are a lot of eccentric people around. Newspapers and magazines are full of stories about people's more unusual behaviour. A person who takes all their clothes off and streaks across a football pitch might have done it for a bet, because he was drunk or just because he wanted to be in the limelight for once. But if he keeps on taking his clothes off in public, he might find himself receiving psychiatric treatment.

Perhaps that's where we draw the line. We put up with odd behaviour so long as it doesn't:
- interfere with other people's lives too much;
- cause danger to anyone;
- make it impossible for the individual to go on living in society, because they are so unhappy or because they have lost touch completely with the real world.

If the behaviour interferes with other people's lives and the individual refuses to or cannot control it, if it is dangerous, or if it makes it impossible for the individual to go on coping with daily life, then it is regarded as mental illness.

⊕ In groups

If people behave oddly should we just let them?

Talk about eccentricity and mental illness. What do you think is the difference?

You and other people – people with mental illnesses

Understanding depression

Depression can mean many different things, because there are different levels of depression. If you are going through a bad patch you may suffer from a mild form of depression. It makes you feel low, but it doesn't stop you from doing everyday things, although everything may seem harder to do and less worthwhile.

A person with severe depression feels a sense of utter hopelessness and that life is so pointless it's not worth doing anything. These feelings are so strong that they make it difficult for the person to cope with life. Their school work may suffer. They may stop wanting to see their friends. They may stop getting up in the morning and keep bursting into tears. They may even contemplate committing suicide.

Don't do it!

Just a couple of words on running away or suicide – *forget it!* Doing a runner is an admission of defeat – not being able to solve the problem that caused the depression. Ironically, it would cause far more problems and probably worse ones.

What does it do to the family? Puts them through torture that could only be described as an anxiety nightmare.

As for suicide, *no* problem is unsolvable. *No* problem is so tangled it can't be unwound.

Teenagers have a whole exciting life ahead. If you get a wonderful partner, beautiful children, a home to be happy in, a challenging job – nobody would want to *miss* all that!

If you or anyone you know shows signs of leaving home or committing suicide, get help at once from some trusted adult.

From *Bad Hair Day* by Nancy Scott Cameron

Symptoms of depression

These are some of the things you may experience if you are depressed:

- ▼ Disliking or even hating yourself.
- ▼ Being preoccupied with negative thoughts and seeing the worst in everything.
- ▼ Rather than feeling alive with anger or grief you are more likely to feel numb, empty and despondent.
- ▼ Blaming yourself and feeling unnecessarily guilty about things.
- ▼ Finding it an effort to do the simplest tasks. You may also be unusually irritable and impatient.
- ▼ You may wake up early in the mornings and not be able to go back to sleep, or you may sleep for longer than usual.
- ▼ You stuff yourself with food and put on weight, or not bother to eat properly and lose weight.
- ▼ Using more tobacco, alcohol or other drugs than usual.
- ▼ Cutting yourself off from others rather than asking for help.

From *Understanding Depression*

What you may be depressed about
by John Coleman

Depression among teenagers might focus on their body, on their physical shape and size. You may hate the way you look and you may be convinced that you are ugly, or that you can never be loved because of your physical appearance.

Perhaps you feel that you cannot make friends and that you are continually excluded from what is going on around you.

You may feel so awkward and tense when you are with others that the idea of a good relationship with someone you care for seems like an impossible dream.

Work or study may seem a waste of time; you may be convinced that you will never achieve anything and that trying to do your best is therefore pointless.

Lastly, you may feel that time is an enemy; it may seem to you that the future will never come – that you wait and wait but nothing ever seems to happen. You may believe that you are condemned to be a child for ever, never allowed to grow up and be the person you really want to be.

From *Moods and Feelings* by John Coleman

✚ In groups

1 What do you learn from this page about the symptoms of depression? How can you tell whether a friend is depressed?

2 What things does John Coleman suggest cause teenagers to get depressed? What other causes of depression can you suggest?

Dealing with depression

How to Defeat Depression

Depression has two important characteristics which you need to be aware of when thinking about what you can do to defeat it:

- It can feed on itself: you get depressed and then you get more depressed about being depressed.
- It can occupy enormous amounts of your time and attention.

Being in a state of depression can then itself become a bigger problem than the difficulties which caused it in the first place. It is important to break the hold depression has on you. Dwelling on difficulties (unless you are thinking constructively) does not help you to solve them. Try to notice when you are doing it and replace that activity with one of those suggested here:

- Find things to do that are so interesting to you that, at least for a while, you forget you are depressed.
- Stop being over-concerned with what goes on 'in your head'. Be physical: walk, run, dance, cycle, play a sport.
- Do anything which will make you laugh.

You need to do things which will make you feel better about yourself. Try and treat yourself kindly and act as if you do feel good about yourself. If you do that your negative feelings will change. Here are some ideas:

- Look after yourself physically: do not abuse your body with drugs, eat well and get exercise.
- Pay attention to your appearance and the place you live. Try and make them more how you want them to be.
- Try and take a break from your usual routine.

You need to deal with anything that is wrong in your life. Important principles to bear in mind are:

- Ask for help. Other people can listen and help you think things through.
- Act rather than be passive. Do not let fear stop you from making necessary changes.
- Do not sit on your feelings. If you need to cry, cry. If you need to get angry, get angry.

These suggestions may seem as if they are a waste of time or too difficult to take up. But when you are depressed it is best not to be guided by your negative feelings. Do your best to try them anyway and you may be pleased with the results.

You may find that what you can do for yourself, and with the support of your family and friends, is not enough. Help is available from elsewhere.

I'm feeling so depressed

Dear Erica:

I feel so low and depressed all the time over nothing in particular. Things are OK so far as my schoolwork is concerned. I don't have any close friends though – at breaktime I hang around with some other girls in my year, but they're not real mates. I've got a boyfriend but we only see each other every now and then, and we're not that serious. He spends a lot of his time going to football training and he seems more in love with his football than he is with me.

I can't really talk to my mum because she doesn't seem to understand and keeps telling me to snap out of it. And my dad's never there – he's either working or down the pub.

Please tell me why I feel so upset that sometimes all I want to do is cry. I'm beginning to feel desperate.

Nicole

Erica says:

It can be tough when you're growing up. As you go through puberty it's not only that your body changes, your feelings are affected too. Because your hormones are working overtime, it can make you feel moody, depressed and generally dissatisfied. Lots of other teenagers feel the way you do.

There are several things you can do to help yourself feel less depressed. Try to focus on the things that are going well in your life and do something about those that aren't going so well. Don't depend on your boyfriend for your social life. It sounds as if he's got other things on his mind. Fix up to see some of your classmates out of school and get to know some of them better. You could broaden your range of friends by joining some after-school clubs.

As far as your family is concerned, many teenagers feel their parents don't understand them. If you really can't get through to them about how you're feeling, try talking to another adult you can trust – perhaps a teacher, or another relative, such as a grandparent. Or you could ring a helpline. Talking things through should help you to put things in perspective and see that your life isn't all gloom and doom. Developing a positive attitude will help you beat those teenage blues.

In groups

Discuss what you learn from this page about what you can do to help you deal with depression.

for your file

Write an article for a teenage magazine about depression, its causes and how to deal with it.

19 You and global issues – poverty

Poverty in the UK

What is poverty?

Poverty means being so poor that you do not have enough money or material possessions to be able to provide yourself with the basic things you need to survive, such as food, water, clothing and shelter. A person who cannot meet such basic needs is in a condition of **absolute poverty**.

In the past, some of the poorest people in Britain lived in absolute poverty. Today, the welfare state aims to provide benefits that will enable everyone in the UK to meet their basic needs. However, there are still large numbers of people whose standard of living is regarded as below what is acceptable in a modern industrial society. Such people live in **relative poverty** compared to the other members of our society.

In theory, in modern Britain, there are sufficient goods and services to provide everyone with a reasonable standard of living. That poverty continues to exist is not due to a lack of wealth, but rather to how that wealth is distributed.

Some people resort to begging to get money to provide their basic needs

Gap between rich and poor has grown

The gap between the rich and the poor in Britain continued to grow through the 1990s, according to a report on social inequalities published by the office of national statistics.

The report highlights the scale of the social justice problem, with April 1998 figures showing that about 3 million children were still living below the poverty line in families with incomes of less than 60% of the median – the middle value – income.

The report shows that the distribution of wealth has altered little in the past 20 years and is even more unevenly distributed. In 1996 1% of the population owned 20% of the wealth. Over half the total wealth was owned by 10% of the population. In the same year, the wealthiest 50% owned almost all the wealth – 93%.

From *The Guardian*, 11 May 2000

In groups

'The government should do more to help the poor. Rich people should have to pay more taxes so that benefits for poorer people, such as the state pension for older people, could be increased.'

Say why you agree or disagree with this view.

Who are the poor?

Low-paid workers Although the government has introduced a minimum wage, many workers still earn a lot less than the average wage. People in unskilled, temporary or part-time work are often poor compared to most other people.

The long-term sick and people with disabilities Over 600,000 people are prevented from working by ill-health. People who have to rely on disability benefits receive less than most people who are working. In addition, they may have extra expenses.

Older people Many older people whose only income is the state pension and other benefits are poor by comparison with the majority of the population.

Carers There are over one million people who work at home looking after either young children or elderly or sick relatives. The majority of them are women. Although they may receive some state benefits, their income is usually much lower than it would be if they worked.

The homeless People who are homeless find themselves caught in a poverty trap. Many employers are reluctant to employ someone who has no permanent home because they are concerned that it might affect their work.

Street life

Homelessness is growing. And the people sleeping on the streets are only the tip of the iceberg. Emily Moore asks what can be done.

Every night up to 2000 homeless people in the UK sleep on the streets. The government wants to see that number cut by two-thirds by the year 2002. How can the problem be solved? In November 1999 Louise Casey, the head of the Rough Sleepers' Unit, caused controversy by saying that giving out hot soup and sleeping bags actually encouraged people to sleep rough. Most charities agree that long-term solutions are most important, but that emergency-based services save lives, especially in winter.

Is homelessness a big problem in the UK?

Yes. Over 10,000 people will sleep rough over the course of a year; 25% of them are aged between 18 and 25 and 90% are male. People who sleep rough are more than 50 times likely to die from violent assault than the general population and are 35 times more likely to commit suicide. Half the people who sleep rough have a bad alcohol problem and 20% misuse drugs.

Do all homeless people sleep on the streets?

No. Street homelessness is just the tiny tip of a huge iceberg. Hundreds of thousands of people live in hostels and bed and breakfasts, or in overcrowded, damp or unsafe housing. Some of these will end up spending time sleeping on the streets. There are around 400,000 people in England who are recognised by their local authorities as officially homeless. However, there are many more 'hidden' homeless, people who are not officially recognised as homeless. At least 41,000 people live in hostels or squats and 78,000 couples or lone parents must share accommodation because they cannot afford to set up home on their own. Centrepoint, the housing agency for young people, estimates that 200,000 to 300,000 young people in the UK (16- to 25-year-olds) are living on friends' floors, in hostels, squats or on the streets.

What causes homelessness?

The homeless charity Shelter believes the underlying reason in general is lack of affordable housing. People sleeping on the street are the most visible face of homelessness and have the most extreme problems. Street homelessness can be caused by family breakdown, domestic violence, drug or alcohol problems and mental illness. Family breakdown is cited by 38% of homeless people as the key factor that first drove them to sleep rough. According to surveys, only one in five of those who sleep rough do so by choice.

Most people sleeping on the streets have troubled backgrounds and need special help. Young people flee troubled homes and move to a new city, to find no room in a hostel and no choice but to sleep on the street. Of the young homeless, 86% have been forced to leave home. One in five street homeless have a serious mental health problem.

Is there a solution to street homelessness?

There are many problems and many solutions. Long-term solutions include providing more affordable, secure, good-quality housing. But handing someone the key to a council flat is not enough. The street homeless need long-term support, for example with alcohol, drug and mental health problems.

Prevention is better than cure. This means providing more support for vulnerable people *before* they end up on the streets.

Adapted from *The Guardian*, 23 November 1999

In groups

Study the article on homelessness, then discuss these questions.

1 How would you define homelessness?
2 'Homeless people have only got themselves to blame.' Say why you agree or disagree with this statement. What are the main causes of homelessness?
3 What can be done to solve the problem of homelessness? Draft a letter to the government suggesting what you think it should be doing to reduce homelessness.

for your file

Imagine you are a homeless teenager. What would it be like to live on the street? Think about the dangers you would face, as well as the difficulty of keeping warm and dry and getting enough to eat. Explain how you became homeless and write about what life is like for you.

You and global issues – poverty

World poverty – the rich–poor divide

The world can be divided into rich countries, where most of the population have a reasonable standard of living, and poor countries, where large numbers of people live in poverty.

Because the majority of the rich countries are in the northern hemisphere, they are often called the North or the developed world. The poor countries are called the South or the developing world. The world's poor countries are also sometimes referred to as the Third World.

Differences between the North and the South

The North	The South
Has 25% of the world's population	Has 75% of the world's population
Consumes 60% of the world's food	25% of the people are hungry or malnourished
Average life expectancy: 73 years	Average life expectancy: 50 years
Low infant mortality rate	High death rate for children under 5
Access to education and health care for all	Limited access to education and health care
Has 80% of the world's wealth	Average incomes are 18% lower than in the North
Highly industrialised: produces 90% of the world's industrialised goods	Limited industrialisation: many people work on the land and live in poverty
Well-developed infrastructures (e.g. transport/communications systems)	Less developed infrastructures

▲▲▲▲ Worlds apart from birth ▼▼▼▼

- In Britain the mortality rate for children under 12 months is 6 per 1000 live births. *In Niger it is 191 per 1000.*
- Every child in this country has access to safe, clean water. *Just 12% of Afghan children enjoy this basic human right.*
- Immunisation against the six major child-killing diseases (measles, diphtheria, tetanus, polio, tuberculosis and whooping cough) has been available to every child in Britain since 1968. *In Chad, fewer than 20% of children under 12 months old have this vital protection.*
- Life-threatening malnutrition is almost unheard of in Britain. *In the developing world over half of the 14 million deaths of children under 5 are either directly or indirectly attributable to malnutrition.*

From *Childmatters*, UNICEF

Education and Poverty

Education and poverty are closely related. In many developing countries, people choose to move to cities to find work. However, without a formal education, many of them cannot find a job. This forces them into shanty towns – dwellings on the edge of cities without a clean water supply or proper sanitation. Without an adequate health education, they may not understand the risks of living in such an area.

Poverty also causes a lack of education. Without resources, schools cannot be built, nor teachers paid to teach. In Mali, in Africa, the average size of a class is 66 pupils. Many children do not receive a proper primary or secondary education.

The result is a vicious circle: without education, a country cannot climb out of poverty, but while poverty still exists, education cannot be provided to much of the population.

From *Global Concerns* by Simon Foster

⊕ In groups

1 What are the main differences between the countries of the North and the countries of the South?

2 How are education and poverty linked?

3 Discuss how different your life would be if you were living in a shanty town on the outskirts of a city in a developing country.

World's poor suffer as the rich destroy our planet

The world's wealthiest people are destroying the planet and causing widespread misery for the poor.

Although they make up just over 10 per cent of the population, individuals living in western industrial countries are responsible for the excessive consumption of half the world's goods and services, according to a new report.

This is having a massive detrimental effect on the environment by causing disasters such as floods and landslides that destroy millions of lives in poorer nations.

The Vital Signs survey, which looks at emerging world trends, found that the enormous gap in wealth, power, opportunity and survival prospects among the world's people is playing a major role in the destruction of the environment.

Although the world economy produced nearly £26 trillion worth of goods and services in 1999, 45 per cent of the income went to the 12 per cent of the world's people who live in western industrial countries.

Author Molly Sheehan, from Worldwatch, said: 'This wealthy minority is largely responsible for the excessive consumption that drives environmental decline. For example, paper use in industrial nations is nine times higher than in developing countries.

'The number of cars per person is about 100 times higher in North America, Western Europe and Japan than in India or China. Third World debt hit a new high of £1.5 trillion in 1999, with some of the world's poorest nations devoting 30 per cent of their national budgets to debt servicing.

'Developing countries are also more vulnerable to environmental change, such as the devastating floods and landslides in Venezuela in December 1999. Worsened by deforestation, this disaster killed more than 30,000 people.'

Other dire predictions in the report are that the world's water supplies are deteriorating rapidly because people are using at least 160 billion cubic metres of water more than they should be every year.

Consumption in the North causes environmental decline in the South

From the *Daily Express*, 31 May 2000

In groups

Imagine you are the members of a government advisory body whose task is to suggest measures that will make people cut down the consumption that is causing environmental decline. Discuss ways of persuading people to cut their consumption, such as restricting the ownership of motor vehicles to essential users, introducing the rationing of vital commodities such as oil and water or introducing a range of 'green taxes'. Draft a statement outlining your proposals and share your ideas in a class discussion.

You and global issues – poverty

In many countries, governments are trying to end the poverty that people face. However, this is not as easy as it sounds. Debt and the world trade system work together to prolong the rich–poor divide.

One way to end the poverty in the South would be if the North allowed poorer countries to escape from the burden of debt. The rich–poor divide would also be lessened if countries in the South were paid a better price for the raw materials that they produce.

Aid <<<<<<<<<

Aid is a weapon in the fight against poverty. Most aid to the South is provided by governments in the North. But how is it used and who usually benefits? Government aid is usually **tied aid**, which means that there are conditions restricting the way it can be used. For example, a country that is given agricultural aid may be told to use the money to buy a certain type of tractor produced in the North. The tractor might not be the best for local conditions; it might be expensive to run, and local farm labourers might lose their jobs if machinery takes over. The country that receives aid may also have to use the skills of foreign experts, even though local people can do the job just as well. In this way, donor countries benefit from giving aid.

Sometimes expensive aid projects do not help the poorest people. For example, dams built with aid money may provide power and store water for irrigation. But the poor, who have lost their land, are unlikely to share in the benefits of modern technology.

How can we end the rich–poor divide?

However, it would be wrong to dismiss all aid. Many aid agencies, such as Oxfam, fill the gaps that are left by governments. The amount of aid they give is small in comparison, but it goes a long way. Aid agencies work to help poor people help themselves.

In Bangladesh, it is unusual for women to go out to work, so it is hard for them to earn money. Local organisations, with help from aid agencies, have set up co-operatives so that they can make a living in their own homes. Thousands of women are weaving bags, mats and hanging baskets from jute, a strong natural fibre that grows in Bangladesh. The women's work has helped them escape poverty. They have also gained independence and confidence.

Other solutions <<<<<<<<<

Other solutions have been suggested to end the rich–poor divide between countries. One of these is to share out wealth by taxation. The United Nations has suggested that the richest countries pay a tax of 0.1 per cent of their Gross National Product. This would be enough to provide basic health care and safe drinking water to all the world's people.

There are many possible answers to the rich–poor divide. But none of them will work unless there is a willingness to share. And that will only come about when individuals and countries learn to respect one another and listen to each other's needs.

In groups

Discuss how we can build a future without the inequalities that exist between the countries of the North and the South.

for your file

Write a letter to a newspaper or to your MP expressing your views about the rich–poor divide.

Fair trade for a fairer future

What is fair trade?

Fair trade is an alternative trading system designed to protect small farmers in developing countries by guaranteeing them a fair price for their crops. It also provides them with an annual bonus to spend on the development of community projects.

Small farmers in developing countries often rely on the income they get from growing crops such as cocoa, coffee, tea, sugar and banana. The price for these crops is set on world markets and can rise or fall. If the price on the world market falls too low, the farmers can find that it is costing them more to produce the crop than they get for selling it. The fair trade system ensures that the farmers receive a guaranteed price for their crops whatever the world market price.

Guarantees a **better deal** for Third World Producers

Fairtrade

The Fairtrade Mark

How does fair trade work?

Fair trade is administered in Britain by the Fairtrade Foundation. The rules are that the farmers must be small scale, part of a democratic group and work in good social conditions. The Fairtrade Foundation awards a consumer label, the Fairtrade Mark, to products that meet its internationally recognised standards.

The way it works is simple. Small-scale producers supply direct to supermarkets or other companies, cutting out the middlemen. A price, guaranteed to be above what they would traditionally get, is set each year in consultation with the farmers and fair trade organisation.

We, the consumers, pay a little bit more and the farmers also get a 'premium' lump sum depending on how much they sell. One of the conditions is that this money must be invested in social projects or infrastructure that the farmers decide themselves.

One Nicaraguan co-operative selling fair trade coffee to British consumers has invested in schools and a small pension for retired farmers. In Tanzania, some of the money from coffee is going towards improved housing.

There are fair trade schemes in more than 30 countries. For us in Europe it means a penny or two extra on a chocolate bar, cup of tea or jar of honey. But for some of the poorest people in the world, the extra cash can repay itself 1000 times.

Clare Short, the international development secretary, says: 'Consumers are increasingly choosing fair trade products because they're good in quality and help some of the poorest people in the world earn their own living. Fair trade is a creative and dignified way out of poverty for some of the most vulnerable people in the world.'

Adapted from *The Guardian*, 7, 13, 17, 21 December 1999

In groups

1. Discuss what the fair trade system is and how it works.
2. Design and produce a leaflet to explain what fair trade means in order to try to persuade people to change their shopping habits and to look for Fairtrade products.

20 You and your achievements –

Assessing your progress and achievements

The aim of this unit is to help you to think about your progress in Year 9, and to discuss it with your tutor, before writing a statement of your achievements. It also gives you the opportunity to review your study habits before you start your GCSE courses.

Preparing your self-assessment

Draft statements expressing your opinion of what you have achieved in Year 9:

1 Write a comment on your **subjects**, saying what progress you think you have made in each one. Give yourself a grade for effort and progress in each subject, and write down your reasons for each grade.

2 Think about the **key skills** you are developing as a result of the work you do in different subjects – communication skills, numeracy skills, study skills, problem-solving skills, personal and social skills, and ICT skills. Write a comment saying how much progress you have made in the development of each of these skills during the past year.

3 List your most significant achievements this year in the **activities** you take part in both in school and out of school. Include details of events organised by clubs and societies that you belong to, sports activities, drama and musical activities and any school events that you have been involved in.

4 Write a comment on what your **behaviour and attitude** have been like in Year 9. Think about you attendance and punctuality; your behaviour in lessons and around the school; how up-to-date you have been with your work; and whether you have volunteered for things and played a full part in the life of the school.

Discussing your progress

Arrange a meeting with your tutor to discuss your self-assessment. Listen carefully to anything your tutor has to say, and add anything which your tutor thinks you have missed out. Note down any comments they make in which they disagree with you, either because they think you have been too harsh on yourself or because they think that you have overestimated your progress.

Setting targets

Use the meeting with your tutor to set targets for Year 10. Identify those subjects and skills that you need to concentrate on improving in Year 10. Discuss what you need to do and the things you will have to change in order to improve those subjects or skills. Then draw up an action plan which lists the steps you are going to take to achieve your goals.

Recording your achievements

Make any alterations to your statements that you think are necessary as a result of your discussion with your tutor and check that your tutor agrees with the changes. Then put your statements in your record of achievement file.

for your file

Draw up a step-by-step action plan for each of the goals that you and your tutor have agreed as your targets for Year 10.

reviewing your progress

Assessing your study habits

The key to effective studying is good organisation. Before you start your GCSE courses in Year 10, think about how good your study habits are.

Do you plan how to use your time?
Are you good at organising your time so that you can fit in all the things you want to do and still get your schoolwork in on time?
Do you keep a diary or weekly planner?
Do you set aside particular times in the evenings and at weekends to do your homework?
How could you organise the use of your time better in the future?

Have you got a quiet place where you can study?
You need to find a quiet place to study where you won't be disturbed by other members of your family or by the TV.
If you're finding it hard to study at home, is there a library you could go to, or a room at school which you could use, either before or after school?

Are you good at organising how you study?
Do you use your study time as productively as you could? Have you got a routine?
Are you good at prioritising and planning ahead, so that you don't have to do things in a rush before a deadline?
Do you set yourself short-term targets, for example, 'I'll write up the notes and draw the diagram, then I'll have a short break'?
Do you take regular breaks so that your concentration level doesn't drop?

Do you keep your files in order?
Do you always put work in the right folder?
Do you regularly spend time sorting out your files, putting papers in order, making sure that they are each dated and numbered?
Do you use dividers so that you can easily find work on different topics?
Do you always put your files back in the same place when you have finished using them?

How good are your revision skills?
Do you just spend your time reading and re-reading your notes in the hope that you'll learn them?
Or do you use strategies that will help you to pick out the key facts in a topic, for example by marking them with a highlighter?
Do you make revision cards?
Do you have a 'revision buddy' and take it in turns with your friend to test each other on the facts you are learning?

In pairs
On your own write down what you think are the strengths and weaknesses of your study habits. Then discuss with a partner what each of you could do to improve your study habits.

for your file
Write a statement saying whether or not you think you have good study habits and how you aim to improve them in Year 10.

Index

adolescence	6–9
adults	6–7, 20–23
aid	92
AIDS	70–71
Amnesty International	27
anorexia	56–57, 59
arguments	21
arms trade	77
assertiveness	44–47
banks	52–53
bereavement	30–32
brothers and sisters	22, 31
building societies	54–55
bulimia	58
chlamydia	69
community	60–63, 78–81
confidence	46–47
conscientious objectors	26
consequences	18
contraception	68–70
councillors	63
crime	38–43
decisions	16–19
depression	82–87
discrimination	10, 13, 14, 28–29
drugs and drugtaking	34–37
eating disorders	56–59
eccentricity	85
elections	62
environment	74–75, 79–81, 85, 91
fair trade	93
fashion	7
feelings	8–9, 30–33, 82–83, 86–87
freedom	26–27
globalisation	72–73
global warming	74–75
grief	30–32
HIV	70–71
homelessness	89
human rights	24–29
identity	6
image	7, 59
influences	17, 51
internet	73
law	14–15, 38–43
local government	60–63
loss	30–33
magazines	51
manic depression	83
media	48–51, 59, 81
mental illness	82–87
money	52–55
moods	8–9
newsletters	80
newspapers	48–50
pacifists	26
parents	20–22
Pedestrians Association	79
peer pressure	19
political parties	64–67
poverty	88–93
prejudice	10–15, 82
press	48–51
press releases	81
pressure groups	78–81
prisons	40–41
punishment	40–42
racism	10–15
rejection	33
responsibilities	22–23
rich–poor divide	90–93
rights	22, 28–29
safer sex	68–71
saving money	52–55
schizophrenia	83
self-assessment	94
self-esteem	44–47
sex	68–71
shoplifting	39
solvent abuse	35
stereotypes	50
STIs	69–71
stress	85
study habits	95
teenage magazines	51
Third World	90–93
torture	25
transnational corporations	72
United Nations	76–77
values and beliefs	6, 26–27
voting	67
women's rights	28–29
youth action groups	43
youth councils	63